KING OF THE MOUNTAIN:
THE BRUNO FAMILY STORY

Joseph James Bruno

KING OF THE

MOUNTAIN:

THE BRUNO FAMILY STORY

John Hutchison,
Hope you enjoy reading
a slice of my history.
Thank you for Carmen
she's the best,

BRUCE BOYD

Copyright © 2016 by Bruce Boyd, bbucita@aol.com. All rights reserved. This book, in whole or in part, may not be used, reproduced, or quoted in any manner whatsoever without prior permission in writing from the author except in the case of brief quotations within the text of reviews or critical articles.

Any brand-name products mentioned in the text of this book are the trademarks or service marks of the respective companies that own them. The mention of any product in this book constitutes neither an endorsement of the product by the writer or publisher of this book nor an endorsement of this book or its content by the products' owners.

ISBN 978-1-5323-2020-0

Manufactured in the United States of America

KING OF THE MOUNTAIN:
The Bruno Family Story

Table of Contents

Foreword   1

Prologue   5

Chapter 1.   Decisions   9

Chapter 2.   A Journey   35

Chapter 3.   Finding a Way   45

Chapter 4.   Another Journey   67

Chapter 5.   Getting Settled   81

Chapter 6.   Politics   103

Chapter 7.   The New Century   119

Chapter 8.   Troubles   143

Chapter 9.   The "Parade"   167

Chapter 10. The Trials   185

Chapter 11. Escape   199

Chapter 12. Prison   213

Chapter 13. Recaptured   229

Epilogue   233

Sources   238

Letter   239

Family Tree   241

Map of Italy   242

FOREWORD

This is a story, my story.

As a young boy, I was confused about my place in a family of five girls. I was in awe of my Italian relatives who spoke in their native Calabrese with hushed voices at any gathering. While I did not understand at the time, I always felt that our family had come from something special; while at the same time a gray cloud seemed to hover over our lives.

Inside the house, the kitchen, where my grandmother, Nanni, used to take me, was my favorite room. I loved to sit at the kitchen table. Somehow, I felt different in that place. I felt as if I belonged.

Five sisters and an overbearing mother made six women against one small boy in our household. My father, a workaholic, was hardly a part of our household, so I felt that I was left to fend for myself. My sisters had the run of the house and the attention of my mother. I slipped through the hallways and explored the yard, trying to find a place where I would feel I belonged. It never happened.

Then one day I found that place in faraway Kelayres, a small village nestled on Broad Mountain in northeastern Pennsylvania. The town was a warm and cozy place in which I found in my great-grandmother's house, Nonna's house, a place where I could finally breathe freely. My cousin Debbie lived next door in what once had been great-great grandmother's house, Bisnonna's, the first home built by our family in America.

Whenever we visited Nonna, I always ran to claim my place in the sunroom located at the front of the big sturdy Italian-glazed brick house. I lay on the bed I claimed as mine, looking out the window and basking in the sunlight coming through the big windows. Across the street I could see the Immaculate Conception Italian Church looming proudly over the village. Great-great-grandfather, Bisnonno, had built the church and dedicated it to the village.

On the steps in front of that church, just outside my window, the whole village would turn out on Saint Mauro's Day to watch the statue of the saint with flowing pale blue robes leave the church and, carried by six altar boys, descend into the crowd. Everyone would join St. Mauro as he moved, almost floated, through the village streets. The original crowd swelled into a huge parade, moving along the two paved streets and ending at the school playground where the carnival would begin.

Behind the two great side-by-side houses of my family was a huge yard bordered by James Street at the far end, a street named after my great-great-grandfather, James Biaggio Bruno. Alongside the alley and in the far corner of the yard, stood a wooden garage, larger than most houses in the village. It had huge doors that were pulled open after unlatching a block of wood that rested nearby in a cradle-like position.

During my youth, the garage was nearly always empty containing only some old decaying barrels and trunks that no one seemed to care about. I loved to play and daydream there with the smell of the dirt floor and the old dry wood.

The garage had its own story. It had been a school-bus garage for a while and then a bootlegging depot which probably supplied a large area of northeastern Pennsylvania. Between the garage and the main house was a one-level structure which at various times had been a pool hall, saloon and speakeasy. On one side I remember a pizzeria owned by my Aunt Elveda. As a kid, I would clean tables for her so that I could buy CMP sundaes (Chocolate Marshmallow Peanut) whenever I had the craving. On the other side was an apartment. In my youth, those buildings were special places where I went with Nanni several times each summer and felt complete.

Then one day everything changed. When I was six or seven, my cousin and I went to a penny candy shop down the street near the schoolhouse. It was owned by a small elderly Italian woman who spoke with a thick Sicilian accent. The two of us peered through the thick glass of the candy case, trying to decide how to spend our dimes. We would point and tap the glass, and the old woman would pick up the pieces we chose, dropping them one-by-one into a small brown bag. Through the old glass, the woman looked like a fairytale character. When we were ready to pay, she leaned halfway over the counter, putting her right arm on top of my head as she peered down at me. Staring, she said, "I know who you are. You're one of them; you are a Bruno. I can see it. Yes, you have the Bruno eyes."

I remember running out of the shop and up Center Street to my nanni and aunt and telling them that the old lady scared me. I told them what she had said and wanted to know what she meant when she said, "You're one of them; you are a Bruno."

That was the first time I felt something was different in this village, something had happened here that I knew nothing about. The family, headed by Nanni, denied knowing of anything ever happening here that was of any importance. So I, being young, forgot about it and went on enjoying my special place.

I was in college before I ever had that feeling again; the feeling that something had happened in the village that I needed to learn more about. I was visiting in Kelayres one summer when some family and I went to a new pub in nearby Hazleton to have lunch. We noticed that the tables were all laminated with old local newspaper clippings. The table we were seated at had one headline that read, "Kelayres Massacre Trial Begins." The date was 1934. Recognizing the name of my special village in such a tragic headline, I asked what the headline meant. No one seemed to know or wanted to talk about it.

That incident in the restaurant began the decade of research that brought me to tell this story and helped me discover my family's villages in Italy. Bucita in the Cosenza province (Calabria region) is a tiny village set on a mountainside overlooking olive groves and small sheep pastures. Casteltermini in Sicily is a centuries-old mountain mineral springs village in the central highland of the Agrigento province.

I traveled to both of the villages in Italy trying to get a sense of the past. I spent countless hours going over newspapers, books, and historical documents in Pennsylvania, New York, and Italy. In these pages is the story I have created from my research and from many of the memories of my family, Kelayres and Bucita. The story is not intended to be a factual history. I was not living at the time of the events, nor have the people who were living then told me very much, as is the custom among Calabrians and Sicilians. Many of the family's records and copies of pertinent documents have been destroyed. My grandmother (Nanni), Antoinette Marie Bruno, was intent on burying the whole sad story, but it has remained alive inside of me.

My goal in these pages is to show the human side of our story; to show that the family and many others involved were just people wanting their piece of the American dream—gold-paved streets and endless opportunity.

Some of these people were real, some of the events were real, but this is basically a work of fiction, my story.

PROLOGUE

*C*ecilia pulled gently, ever so gently, on the shade's cord, only partially revealing the scene outside the late Packard model car. The two women peeked from their hiding place—wife and daughter of the man they could see being escorted in handcuffs into the cold, dark Eastern State Penitentiary.

The ride in the Packard from their home in Kelayres to this prison fortress just inside Philadelphia had been long and quiet. For both women it had been a time of conflicting thoughts and turmoil. For Antoinette, several agonizing weeks had passed since she had seen her father, Joseph Bruno; for her mother, Cecilia, almost nine long, stressful months had passed since she had seen her beloved husband. For both women it had been weeks and months of not knowing what the outcome would be. Today was truly a day of mixed emotions, but at least now they would know exactly where he was, and in the future could visit him openly—as openly as one could visit an inhabitant of this place with its thick solid stone castle-like walls.

"Ah, this was not the way it was supposed to be, not what Joseph and I had planned for our life, for you children," Cecilia Bruno moaned as she sighed. But on that hot, gray, humid afternoon of the twenty-fourth of August in 1937, this was the way it was turning out.

Antoinette leaned over to take her mother in her arms.

"Oh, Mama, dear Mama!" she barely whispered, gasping for the words that would not come. In her despair, she held her mother tightly.

Through the narrow opening beneath the window shade, the women could see with little joy that Joseph was alright. His proud-as-a-peacock strut was still evident, though somewhat diminished by all he had experienced. His head was still high, and if his heart was heavy and his eyes saddened by the events of the last few months, it was evident only to those who watched from their hiding place, to those who loved him. They wanted to call out to him, run to him, hold him in their arms, and snatch him away from this horrible place, out of this unimaginable dream.

Cecilia had so much to tell him: of her emotional rollercoaster ride over the last months, of the pain of not seeing him for so long, of being unable to embrace him; of no longer having his wonderful scent on their pillows, and no longer being able to remember it during the hours she lay awake and sleepless. The truth was that she could barely manage to keep the family afloat; but that secret would have to remain only with her. Though the bills were still being paid by the huge sums of money that continued to come in as a result of the family's operations, without Joseph's leadership, those, too, were beginning to diminish. Cecilia had so much to say, but she wouldn't say it even if she had the chance. Better to keep it to myself, she thought, as she continued to watch the slow procession of people with her husband, Joseph James Bruno, at its center.

Antoinette wanted to tell her papa that she could hardly sleep. She sat up late every night, thinking, wondering what would come next in this horrible story. How will Papa survive this torment, this dishonor? she wondered.

Dear Mama, Antoinette thought as she took her mother's hand in hers and kissed it. How will you continue to cope with the looks on your friends' faces? They sneer at you when you go to Lotsie the butcher or the IGA grocer; they turn away when they meet you on the street. People laugh at you from the back of the post office when you pick up the mail, some of it with no return address or signature—just hateful, awful words.

Mama is strong and had grown even stronger through all this, but who could bear so much for so long with no end in sight?

So, instead of running to comfort him as any loving mother and daughter would, Antoinette and her mother could only hide behind the shades of the Packard and peer out like church mice in the shadows of the night. Their thoughts were with him, as were their prayers, but they could only hope that he sensed their presence. The place was swarming with reporters. If they saw Joseph look in their direction, if they even noticed them in the car, they would be on them like the pack of dogs they were, hounding them day after day, treating them like animals, with no respect, no thought for their feelings. They would torment them with flashes from their cameras, with endless, intrusive questions, gruesome interviews, a ruthless spinning of lies.

Hiding in the car was the only way for Cecilia and Antoinette to be there for husband and father yet still dodge the ubiquitous press. They could only watch as he disappeared behind the heavy gate into the huge, overpowering stone walls of the massive fortress with its silent towers and expressionless guards. As the massive, iron twelve-foot-high gate slammed shut, a part of the two women was locked inside.

No, this was not the place, not the time for a reunion. That would have to wait until the officials were done with their questioning about the nine months since Joseph's escape. Then, when he was settled in this dreadful place, they could see him again.

Nine months earlier, Joseph Bruno had escaped from that small county jail at the last moment. He had felt he had no choice. Only by fleeing could he manage his operations and survive the pain and humiliation of the accusations flung at him during the long, costly trials. To try to mount a campaign that could untangle him from this nightmare life sentence was his only option.

Joseph also wanted to clear his family name, a well-respected name that he and his brother and cousin, their father and uncles, their grandfather, had worked so hard to establish.

What exactly had happened to make this dreadful day come about?

CHAPTER 1

DECISIONS

James Biaggio Bruno stood looking out over the golden Calabrian mountainside shining in the blinding afternoon sunlight. It was a deceptive gold, as he well knew, for the southern Italian soil was rocky and barren, and the people who farmed it were not well rewarded for their efforts.

His body fit the land, hard and wiry. his arms were knotted with muscles from his work, and his skin was brown, both from his mediterranean Italian blood and from the hot sun.

But, rough as the country was, difficult as the life there was, this was his home, his family's home, and it had been for generations. It was not just his parents and brothers and sisters, his grandparents, but his aunts and uncles, cousins, great-uncles and great-aunts, second cousins, cousins by marriage—too many to name. they joked about being related to everyone in the village—and half of the next village. you always knew you could get help with your problems because the family was always there.

But there was only so much the family could do when life was so hard, when everyone had to struggle for every little bit, every bite of food, every tool, every scrap of clothing.

Biaggio's family, like most of the people living in the poor remote region of southernmost Italy, prayed and asked throughout the generations, "Why? Why did it always have to be so hard?"

But Biaggio was not like that. He believed that life had more in store for him than just hardship, and he set out to change things. He was sharp, smart, and strong, and he knew how to use his strengths.

When James Biaggio Bruno was born in 1855, Austria ruled the Italian Peninsula, having quelled the short-lived revolutions of 1848 and 1849. But the fight for Italian independence was not over by any means, as various revolutionary heroes plotted and fought with more or less success.

News of political activities reached the Bruno family and their neighbors slowly, long after they had come to pass, and far too late to do anything about them. That made it easy for the people to be drawn into a sense of hopelessness and helplessness. A mentality of defeat emerged amongst the Calabrians; it seemed there was nothing they could do about any of the forces that controlled their countryside and daily life. No one from the outside took an interest in the area, because there was nothing in this remote mountainous land to interest them. No one in the area itself took an interest, either, because there seemed to be no possibility of change. The inhabitants would simply get by with what the family and village could provide from the work of their backs. The only one who possibly listened was the Savior, but he never really answered their prayers.

At this time, they needed men to step up and lead. Men such as Guiseppe Garibaldi, who led an army from the southern island of Sicily north to Naples to run the Austrians out of the north, and Victor Emanuel, who marched through the south to rid the lower peninsula of its Bourbon rulers, were considered heroes. But even so, these heroes did not change the Calabrian way of life much. Victor Emanuel marched through the area, but he did little in the region to change anything. He was simply heading south, passing through an unimportant province in the grand scheme of the revolution. Calabria was poor—it had always been poor—an agricultural region divided by mountains and isolated from the north and its cities and markets by dialect and distance. Nothing much changed there, not at first anyway. But then others began to come around talking about land for sale, the common land, the grazing land, where the Brunos and their neighbors had grazed their sheep and cattle for hundreds of years.

The only ones able to buy these lands were those who already had land, who had money, and they just became wealthier. In time those wealthy landowners began to work to keep people from using what had once been common lands. It took them a little while to get organized, to hire men to work for them, to enforce the new restrictions, to guard the new boundaries, but when they did, the peasants' world began to shrink. Life became even more difficult, with less land to till and to use for grazing their sheep. This, of course, caused more hunger and despair, along with less freedom and fewer opportunities for the peasants.

In 1860 rumors again flew about great events far to the north in the cities, in distant, magnificent, mythological Roma. Someone named Count Cavour had got together with Napoleon III, the nephew of the old banished emperor, and together they had chased the Austrians back over the Alps and proclaimed independence. They called their new country the Kingdom of Italy, united for the first time in its history, and in 1861, they crowned Victor Emanuel II king.

Biaggio lived with his parents, Luigi and Maria Lucia in the tiny village of Bucita on Via Castil overlooking the olive groves of the Catena Costiera Mountains. San Fili was actually the closest place resembling a town, and it could be seen across the valley with its large cathedral guarding the region and reminding the people, lest they forget, who still controlled their daily lives. Despite Cavour, Napoleon III, and whatever happened in Roma, it was the Church that dictated their futures. It was the Church that listened but did not answer their prayers.

In 1862 The Brunos' little world included a city called Cosenza, a tough three-hour hike from the seaport of Paola, on the arching top of the foot of the great kicking boot of Italy. All of this was a small slice of the rocky, barren, sunny province with the musical name of Calabria. And Bucita was perched on the mountainside right in the middle of this isolated world.

Biaggio had two brothers, Francesco (Frank), at eight almost a year older, and Pietro (Peter), several years younger. Biaggio's best friend Antonio lived a few houses down on the dusty Via Castil, and he had two brothers, as well. Biaggio had two sisters, Tomasina and Carmela who were mostly pious little girls, struggling to be neat and pretty in a dirty, rough world— although all those brothers were a big part of the problem.

Together the boys ran and fought and worked and played from sunup until sundown, and as much of the night as they could get away with. They were lean from too little to eat, too much work, and the sheer exuberance of youth.

Biaggio's mother, Maria Lucia, was always busy with cooking, trying to keep enough clothes on the family's backs, and tending the children and Papa's old father, Blazius, who lived with them. Mama and the other women of the village would also go gleaning in the fields of the big farms, sometimes collecting more grain than they could grow themselves. They would use the grain to make bread and pasta, the staples of their meager existence.

Biaggio's father, Luigi, worked long hours in the groves, traveling back and forth from their house to where they farmed and kept their animals, to where they cut firewood, or to the river or the sea at Paola for fishing, which added some welcomed variety to their tables. The family's crop was olives, as was the case for most of the villagers, and each family also raised most of their own vegetables—tomatoes, broccoli, escarole, zucchini, beans, and herbs such as basil, oregano, and garlic to season otherwise dull lives. Nonna Tomasina, who had died young, always said if you had these three herbs and some salt, you could make anything taste wonderful.

Almost every family had a small vineyard where they tended their grapes to make the fabulous wines that flowed through their veins. The Bruno family was more fortunate than most. They had a mule and shared a small herd of sheep and goats with neighboring families. The goats and sheep were kept for milk, which was used to make the tasty cheeses they all enjoyed.

But life was never easy in Calabria. Government was non-existent, the Church controlled life, and the weather was always a problem.

Schools were another problem the region had faced since the rebellion. The south was of little consequence to the new government because of its poverty, lack of political and strategic influence, and physical isolation, so the government didn't even bother to support education. To fill the gap, the Church set up schools. As often as not, the teachers in the school were the local priest or an itinerant brother who would tell the students their version of history, of the traitorous barbarians who took over the country and stole Rome from the sacred holy Church. Nevertheless Biaggio and Frank did well with their studies, their active, inquisitive minds always asking for more, for better explanations. They wanted to know all about the heroes of history, the conquerors. Peter, on the other hand, liked school because it was easier than working in the fields. Village parents still demanded that the children be let out early to help with work. They let them go to school when weather kept them out of the fields.

Biaggio quickly learned to read, and only a little less quickly to write. He pestered the priest-teacher to loan him books of history, even religious history, if that was all he could get. He loved biographies, geography, and history. The Church, of course, offered nothing heretical, and it was only later that Biaggio began to question what was written in these books. He also heard another side of the stories from travelers, young men who'd been to the north, who'd been in the war. They told glorious tales of victorious independence, of wresting their freedom with their bare hands from foreigners, the Austrians, and from the confining, suffocating hands of the Church.

Who was a boy to believe? The massive stone church was there, looming over the valley and the village, while the travelers with their stories came and went.

Revolutions and their tales were a distant concern for the people of Calabria in the late 1800s. They had other problems that directly affected their daily lives. Problems such as the epidemics that had been coming far too frequently in recent years, each time claiming more and more loved ones. Sometimes it felt as if the region were doomed to be poor and isolated, always with some kind of disease, flood, or drought trying to destroy the hard-working families that were barely hanging on.

The children had to work in the fields with the adults. At lunchtime, while breaking the fresh bread Mama had packed and passing it around with cheese and prosciutto, the men would take turns telling stories, history disguised as adventure, stories of Guiseppe Garibaldi and the Red Shirt Army, the famous Thousand Volunteers, designed to brighten an otherwise drab, exhausting day of laboring in the fields.

On the long walk back home from the fields, the parents and elders would inch along slowly, tired and sore from the long hours of hard work. At first the children walked slowly, as well, but soon youthful exuberance took over and they began to run and play on the edges of the dirt road. Biaggio always wanted to be Guiseppe Garibaldi riding on his tall horse and leading the Red Shirts just like in the lunchtime stories.

"I am Garibaldi! I am Garibaldi!" Biaggio ran into the road, clutching a big stick as a rifle, a scrap of red cloth tied around his neck. "I am a red shirt!"

"You always say that! Let me be Garibaldi for once!" Frank ran after him, his fists raised to defend his claim.

"No! I am the leader!"

"You are not!" Frank pushed Biaggio down and took the rifle and pointed it at his chest.

"All right, you be Garibaldi today. There's no need to get angry."

Frank released his hold on Biaggio, who immediately jumped up and grabbed the rifle back from his brother's hands.

"I am Garibaldi!" he shouted, running off toward where Antonio and the others were running ahead. Frank stood in the dust scowling, his hands again in fists.

Nonno, their grandfather Blazius, called out, "Biaggio! Come back here!" Biaggio, the childhood nickname, would stay with him throughout his life, long after Nonno was at rest in the San Fili churchyard vault.

Biaggio slowly came back up the road, the triumphant grin gone from his face.

"Yes, Nonno?"

Biaggio's grandfather stood with a hand gripped firmly on each boy's shoulder.

"You are fine, strong, proud boys, and that is good. But you must never fight with your own brother, or trick him. Your family is the most important part of life. Your family is everything."

"*Sì*, Nonno, *sì*," Biaggio hung his head in shame, sudden tears streaking his dirty face, raising little clouds of dust as they hit the ground. Only Nonno could bring him down with his gentle way.

"What do you say to your brother, Biaggio?"

Biaggio sniffed, wiped his tears with the back of an even dirtier hand, and turned to his brother. "Franco, Franco, *mi fratello, mi dispiace*, I am sorry! *Scusi, per favore, scusi!*"

He thrust the toy gun urgently into his brother's hands, willing him to forgive him, to absolve him in front of Nonno. Wise Nonno was always right; family would always mean survival.

"You be Garibaldi, I'll be Giuseppe Mazzini. *Roma o morte!*" Biaggio now insisted.

Emotions ebbed and flowed through Biaggio like clouds on a spring morning, first anger, then joy, sorrow, shame, and grief, suddenly overwhelming him, then gone, forgotten in the time it took him to turn around.

Despite the hard times, something was very wonderful about sitting at the old, creaking wooden table Nonno had made. On Sundays at Via Castil, the whole family, dressed in their church clothes and, smiling, would be found there eating, talking, drinking wine, and enjoying what they had—each other. It was hard to feel bad on Sunday—they got to rest, they got enough to eat (sometimes), and they got to drink wine.

In many ways, the wine was the family. Everyone helped create the wine. From the exhausting tending of the vines to the festive crushing of the grapes, everyone in the family put their blood into the wine. Zio Filippo would start to play his fiddle and Antonio's papa would come in with his accordion. Then Zia Isabella would take Biaggio's hand and start to spin him around the floor, and soon Mama would be up and dancing and laughing and kicking up her long skirts in such a way they couldn't believe it was Mama. Then someone would bring another bottle of wine that they'd kept hidden away for a special occasion, and soon the stars were coming out and the little ones were asleep in the corners or on laps, and the dances would change to lullabies. Even though Biaggio thought of himself as a big boy, he still sat on the floor next to Mama and leaned on her legs and nodded his head in time with the eerie wailing violin. The next thing he knew, Papa was carrying him to bed, and then it was Monday morning and life crept back to normal, as if it had all been a wonderful dream.

The festival days were Biaggio's favorite times. He could forget the troubles of the world when he was praying and singing and walking in the festival parade. Jesus was going to come, and he would help everyone. And the meek would inherit the earth, at least for a day.

So there were plenty of festivals—for the patron saints of each town and village, for holidays, birthdays, weddings, funerals, the olive harvests. The people clung to any chance to laugh and dance and forget for a short time.

The patron saint of Bucita was Saint Biaggio, so of course, that festival was Biaggio's favorite. It would go on for several days, with parades and special masses and delicious food, dancing, singing, music, and more food. Ah, the food! Cannelloni, painstakingly hand rolled and filled by Mama, was stuffed to perfection overflowing with the spinach and cheese from the family's fields and livestock. The cannoli and gelato for dessert along with Limoncello, were also products of the family kitchen. The kitchen, of course, was across the narrow alley behind the rest of the house so the heat of the oven did not add to the oppressive temperature of the summer. In the winter it was everyone's favorite place to be, with all the activity of the family cooking going on, the warmth and the flickering light to read by. Not to mention that Biaggio would get to taste the sauce and lick the bowls that were sent his way.

He would sigh and say, "I wish every day was a festival day." "Ah, but then they wouldn't be special," Nonno told him.

As much as he trusted him, though, Biaggio wasn't so sure he was right this time.

What Biaggio read in the history books made him begin to question that promise about the meek inheriting the earth. When he looked around the kitchen at what little they had, it didn't appear to him like the meek were getting anything right now. Didn't the Lord help him who helped himself? Biaggio was planning to help himself.

He was strong. He got through his work in the fields in good time, carried a book in his pocket and stopped to read every now and then, hoping Blazius didn't catch him.

But his grandfather wouldn't do anything to Biaggio; he would just smile and say, "Ah, that's my Biaggio, always trying to get ahead." Then he'd nod and take up the slack. Biaggio hated it when that happened. Nonno didn't need any more work; he already worked too hard. Nonno stood about five feet ten inches in height, which was tall for a Calabrian. Now, though, he was a little bent over from age, and he was so thin Biaggio sometimes was afraid he'd blow away when the wind picked up from the coast. He always ate little so that Papa, Mama and the children could have more. When Biaggio watched Nonno walking around the groves, he thought the older man looked like one of the stately cypress trees blowing in that same wind along the Via Castil.

In later years, Biaggio remembered, "In 1869, Mama became ill from the dampness of a cold spring. She was very weak and frail for months. Papa could hardly bear to leave her to go to work in the fields. One day he returned and Mama was gone. She had taken her last breath and left us with Tomasina to run the house."

When the children of the village were young, the priests had told them that bad men had taken over the government. As they got older and started reading the newspapers and hearing about things in ways other than from the priests, they found out that the Church and the Pope were still angry that anyone had taken Rome away from the Church and had separated the Church from the government. Biaggio learned that the Pope had forbidden members of the Catholic Church to vote—just a few at that time, true, since only the wealthy, the land owners, just a fraction of the population of Italy, could vote then. But even of those few, most ignored the Pope's decree and voted anyway. How could they not? The Church was important, yes, but government was every day, was everything, was money and land and power. In the same way that the Church listened but did not answer, the government answered but did not listen. The laws were punitive and hurt the people who had the least.

When Biaggio was almost twenty, the Church began to select people in the town to perform various civic duties. They called the people the *laity*, and they told the local people to come to these representatives when they had problems. This was the Church's attempt to circumvent the government, and it caused confusion among the people, who wondered who was in charge, whom they could trust, and to whom they should go. The Church was encouraging them to doubt the government, to disrespect government officials, to do what they could get away with, which was in blatant disregard for the government's position of separation of church and state.

Children growing up during this period had a hard time with discipline, with understanding or relating to respect and rules. The young people didn't know what to do or whom to trust.

Biaggio became more and more confused. As far back as anyone could remember, like his father, Luigi, and his grandfather, Blazius, the Church was family, like parents. And now he was finding out that the priests had not always told the truth, certainly not all of it anyway, and that men did what they wanted to do, just as they always had. It was a constant struggle for control, for power over other people, for wealth. It was as if a man who had the most land or money could, if he was clever enough, take control.

And still life in their village got harder. The people were paid less and less for what they raised. Someone said people could buy things from other countries cheaper than they could buy from their own countrymen. How could that be?

Some of the people from the town moved away, to France or Spain—anywhere to get away from the sickness, the starvation. Sometimes the priests would say that it wouldn't do them any good to go someplace else, because people were having the same problems everywhere. In this way many stayed rooted right where they were, afraid of the unknown, listening only to the Church.

In order to survive, the people had to grow more of their own food. They needed more cleared fields. Those who owned land with trees on it were cutting them down as fast as they could and had been for years now. But in a very short time that land became a horrible wasteland—arid, barren, and dry with the winter droughts. Then all the fields' growth eroded in the heavy spring rains. All the top soil washed away, and the freshly planted crops with it. Some years the rivers in the lowlands would rise out of their banks, and the flooding would wash away houses, even whole villages. In Bucita, high in the Catena Costiera Mountains, they didn't have to worry about flooding, but the erosion of their farmlands and olive groves was devastating.

There was also the sickness that would come—malaria—, and people would die so fast that the living ones couldn't get the dead ones out of the house to the cemetery, couldn't get away from the cursed sickness. Then they would die, too. So many people—just gone.

Eventually news started coming to Calabria about the Americas, lands far, far away, across oceans so wide it took weeks to cross them. How could all this be true? What sort of man could have gone that far away to discover those countries? Who would have been brave enough? Foolish enough? How could you live long enough to get there? How could you carry enough food and water with you to get that far? Biaggio remembered the geography book he had read and how unbelievable it had all been.

It sounded like a fairy tale to him, like those stories that Nonna told in the evening to quiet the children after a festival day, her voice soft, almost singing. These were tales of giants and trolls and magical people who could fly, who could change themselves into animals, into birds, who would fly into a village and kill a bad child or rescue a good one and carry him off to a palace with all the food he could ever eat, and wear fine clothes and have a beautiful bride.

America. What a beautiful word. Biaggio would say it over and over under his breath, like a song, a prayer, just as he used to repeat Nonna's words when he was sleepy and full to overflowing with the richness of the day, of the joy of being with God, with Jesus, with Holy Mary. He would be so near to falling asleep, fighting to stay awake so he could hear her whole story even though he'd heard it a thousand times. He knew what would happen, but he wanted to hear it again, how the good boy, the honest boy, who worked so hard in his papa's fields, would be chosen and would become a prince, a king, a rich and happy man.

Soon everyone was talking about America, and the rumors were flying that people from the northern countryside around Naples were going there, to a country called Argentina, or another called Brazil. The ships that brought the fruit were taking people back. Biaggio started looking to the west every chance he got, every time he thought of it.

One Sunday in the spring, Biaggio and Frank woke early in the morning and slipped quietly into their clothes.

"Pietro, do you want to come with us?" Biaggio whispered in the darkened room. Peter lay still in his tousled bed, his black eyes barely opening when Biaggio pulled at his toes.

"What, so early? No, I don't think so, it is the day of rest." Peter yawned.

Fighting their own sleepiness and wiping their eyes open wider, they were full of excitement of the undiscovered. "We are going to see the ocean."

"Ah, well, you go, then, and paint me a picture, sì?" Peter egged them on so he could sleep.

Biaggio laughed, but he knew that Peter would be very interested if they decided to do anything new and exciting. Peter couldn't imagine America by looking at the ocean, but Peter would be the first to board a ship if they were to sail there!

It was barely light, and the air was cool, the ground wet with dew. Biaggio stole half a loaf of Mama's bread along with some cheese and stuffed it into his shirt. They slipped out, met Antonio down the road, and headed for the ocean.

"Mama will never let me forget skipping Mass," Frank said, with only a hint of regret in his voice.

"Yes, there'll be extra chores for us tomorrow!" Biaggio laughed and ran ahead. They'd played in these mountains all their lives, hiking here and there to a favorite spot— here an imaginary fortress, there a castle—battles fought and won, enemies conquered.

The sun was halfway up the mountain when they finally caught sight of the silver shimmer in the distance. They'd been to the sea before, to the fishing village of Paola that hugged the thin strip of land at the base of their mountains. It was a trip that could be made in a day, and several times a year the family did make a day of it, the men fishing, the women resting in the shade, the children playing in the sea. All would enjoy eating the fish, cooked on an open wood fire on the beach, before they started the climb back home.

Although the trail was familiar, this day it was different. The ocean meant freedom to them now, it meant America and riches and fame and power. Biaggio just knew that it would look different, that he would see a shining golden path across the water, pointing the way to anyone who was courageous enough to leap onto it.

By the time they arrived, they were hot and dusty and thirsty, but Biaggio stood still, immobile, gazing into the distance, almost believing if he looked hard enough, long enough, he would see America, would see the shining golden towers of his imagination.

Antonio pulled his arm and said, "Biaggio, come and sit in the shade, it's too hot out here. You're crazy! You can't see America from here!"

Biaggio lingered a moment longer, the picture of America, its towers of light, its streets paved with gold, slowly fading from his dazzled eyes. Then he turned and walked through the dust to the shade of the bent old manzanita tree. There was barely enough shade for the three of them to lie down. Biaggio lay with his head on Frank's hard belly, and his head bounced every time

Frank laughed, which was often, because they were all telling stories and jokes. They savored some oranges they had stolen from a farmer's grove, carefully licking every drop of juice from their fingers. The three boys napped in the shade for a short time, dreaming of America.

Following a week of punishment and extra chores for their adventurous jaunt to the sea, it was time for Antonio's birthday celebration.

"Where's Biaggio?" Antonio asked as Frank and Peter met him in the road.

"Ah, he's home with his book," Peter answered.

Antonio ran out the door in disbelief, shouting, "No! The fool—I'm going to get him."

Almost out of breath when he arrived at Biaggio's house, Antonio shouted through the open window, "It's my birthday! You have to come along, Biaggio! There'll be dancing and food, your two favorite things!"

Looking out the window over the top of the book he was reading, Biaggio shouted back, "There'll be girls, you mean, your favorite thing. No, 'Tonio, not tonight. I want to finish this book before I have to give it back to the priest. You go and kiss them all for me. You're better at it than I am!"

"Pah! You'll never find a wife that way!" Antonio lamented.

"I'll find a wife in America!" Biaggio retorted. "The most important thing is to get there!"

One day, Biaggio was in the big cathedral in Cosenza where he had attended Mass a few times. The early morning light pouring through the colored glass of the windows gave the cathedral an unearthly look, all blue and gold, like heaven, Biaggio thought. On an earlier visit to Cosenza one rainy day, Biaggio had stopped at the cathedral and fallen in love with the peacefulness of its stunning stained glass windows reflecting on the intricate stone work and marble floor. Now he often stopped in on his trips to the city.

Biaggio had taken over the regular family trip to Cosenza to sell cheese and olives to an uncle who owned a small shop in the market area. Before his trip home, Biaggio had to purchase some things the family could not buy in Bucita or San Fili. Biaggio smiled to himself. Tomasina always wanted something that he had to look for, walking from shop to shop, seeking just the right shade of thread or bit of cloth. And today he wanted to get something for Nonno's birthday, something special. So he meandered through the market stalls and shops until he had ended up on the cathedral steps.

On one such stop he had met Stephano, one of the church brothers, and they had begun talking about America. Stephano had traveled and studied in Rome, and Biaggio loved to listen as Stephano brought history and geography to life with his stories. But, oddly, Biaggio became even more confused about his future and the lure of distant lands. Stephano assured him that an education is the best method of finding one's way and offered to lend him some books, to which Biaggio eagerly agreed.

That day Biaggio had finished getting the family's supplies and had stopped to return Brother Stephano's books. The two men sat up until late that night talking of the changes happening in their country and in the world, and Stephano invited him to spend the night in the rectory near the church.

In the morning the two men walked together to Mass. Stephano left Biaggio at the front steps as he was almost late to prepare for the services. The church was nearly empty. Biaggio entered the sanctuary alone and sat far over on the right side. It was very early, but he needed to leave soon to get to home to celebrate Nonno's birthday with his family. The Mass had not yet begun, so he sat looking around—at the windows, at the figure of the Savior hanging on the cross above the altar—but his eyes kept being drawn to the Blessed Virgin, almost in front of him.

The light shining on the face of the statue, a pale pinkish gold, gave her skin such a look of life that Biaggio could almost believe she was breathing, that the hand she held aloft would rise even higher in a blessing on those who prayed to her so often, so fervently, with such passion and compassion. His confusion was gone now, his answer clear as if it came directly from her. *Go to find a better life in a new country, far from the corrupted, arrogant ways of the rulers of this poor old country.*

A new life, a fresh young country, just waiting for strong courageous young men like himself to take it for their own!

Biaggio would remember this morning many times as the years passed, always able to see the beautiful face of the Virgin, the smile on her lips, and to hear her words in his ears.

"Go, Biaggio, go with my blessing."

People were coming into the church now, and someone was walking in front of the statue, so he came back reluctantly to reality. A woman in a white lace mantilla knelt at the altar rail and bent her head. She prayed for a moment then rose and turned, walking to a seat near the front.

She seemed just a girl, but so beautiful Biaggio could hardly bear to look at her. It was as if she was a shining light, a star, an angel come down to earth. But look at her he did, he couldn't resist, at her face faintly flushed from the cool morning air. *How right, how perfect for her to pray to the Blessed Virgin, so lovely, so pure herself, praying to the Purest One,* Biaggio thought. He knew he should stop looking at her, should bend his own head in prayer and respect her privacy. He stole one more glance, and as he did she lifted her long, lovely dark lashes and looked into his eyes.

She was with Biaggio's friend, Giorgio, who also studied with Brother Stephano. Sometimes Brother Stephano would get the two young men together and test them on their knowledge of the world. Biaggio had to work much harder because he had much less education than Giorgio, who came from a well-to-do family. Giorgio's family controlled vast vineyards along the slopes overlooking Cosenza from the west, which enabled him to go to school all of the time instead of working.

After the Mass, Biaggio went up to Giorgio, hoping to be introduced to the young lady. Suddenly, his heart began to pound, his palms were wet, his throat dry. He couldn't speak, couldn't even say good morning to his good friend.

Under her mantilla, the young woman's hair was not heavy and black like all the other girls, but light like the dusky evening sun shining on the Calabrian hills, a red-gold such as he had never seen before. And her skin! So fair, and dusted with light brown freckles. She carefully kept out of the sun to protect her delicate skin and hair. He was entranced by her. He had never seen anyone so lovely.

All Biaggio's confidence vanished at the nearness of this elegant young lady. He managed to stammer a greeting, and his friend Giorgio, laughing to see the usually self-assured Biaggio so nervous and awkward, introduced him to Marie Antonia Abbaté, his cousin from Casteltermini, in the mountainous southern interior of Sicily.

Marie Antonia was taken with Biaggio, too, and she helped put him at ease by joking about Giorgio's accent as the Calabrese speak with a significantly different dialect than the Sicilians. The harsh *ch* sound for *s* and *g* can be very confusing until one puts it all together. Introducing Marie as *Chiglian* instead of *Sicilian* for example, had everyone laughing, but it made Biaggio feel a little less clumsy about hiding his own emotions. Even before her eyes had met his in the church, she had felt his look—the hairs on the back of her neck had stood up as she knelt to pray, and when she had looked up at the Blessed Virgin she had seen the knowing smile on her face.

In 1876, Biaggio had turned twenty-one and was a handsome, golden-skinned man that any woman would naturally desire. His body was well defined in its otherwise compact stature. He stood just over five feet eight inches tall, and every inch was muscle from working the fields.

Giorgio invited him to have dinner with them, and afterward they spent the afternoon in the cool quiet of the garden, talking and laughing, telling stories and singing songs. Biaggio thought he had gone to heaven without the burden of having to die.

He tried everything he could think of to get Marie Antonia alone, but she just as skillfully dodged his advances. He didn't realize at the time that Sicilian custom dictated that an unmarried woman could not be alone with a single man even in the broad daylight of late afternoon. It was unheard of and would shame the family. Biaggio was lucky, actually, because if Marie Antonia's mama had been in town, she would have sat between them during the entire visit and not let Marie's beautiful eyes gaze into his. So he gave up trying, and amid the group asked her about her life. She demurely answered some of his questions, and her cousin answered some of the others. They said she was from near Agrigento on the southern coast of Sicily. Her village was actually up in the surrounding mountains, with a royal sounding name, Castelermini. The old Roman town was actually built around a fine natural hot spring, enjoyed by the aristocracy. Giorgio said that Agrigento and the country around it was very beautiful. He spoke of standing on a mountain above the town, high above the sea, watching the sun sparkle on the waves, the white sand glistening on the beach far below.

Biaggio looked at Marie and imagined standing there with her, her fair hair blazing in the sun, the soft breeze blowing wisps of it around her face, her eyes shining like the sea, the warm springs bubbling behind them so invitingly.

Marie Antonia Abbaté. Such an elegant name, perfect for such an elegant girl. No, not girl, a woman. A woman she was, not like the girls Biaggio knew in his village, but ripe and full. His lips wanted to taste the rich fruit of hers. He had to turn away to hide the flush that came to his face with these thoughts.

Sylvia, Giorgio's sister, asked Marie about the school she attended.

"Is it true that they only spoke *Inglese* there?"

"No, we spoke mostly English, but we also spoke Italian, and we studied Latin and French and a little Greek," Marie answered in her sweet accent.

At this Biaggio turned back to look at her more closely. All this—beauty, elegance, wealth and education, too! Then, the reality of the situation hit him—this girl, this woman, would never dream of loving a man like him. Never! And furthermore, she was Sicilian. He was a poor Calabrese boy from the mountains.

Now he turned his face away in shock, pain and embarrassment. He realized how poorly he was dressed in comparison to these young people from the town, and he felt a fool. But it was no use; he had to look at her. She was looking at him, as if sensing his discomfort, and she smiled at him, which added to his desire to know her even better.

Then Giorgio and Sylvia's mother called them into the house for a dessert of grapes and cheese, and Biaggio knew it was time for him to leave. He had no choice but to say good-bye to all of them together. He could not even get next to Marie Antonia.

Biaggio's heart and mind were in turmoil as he walked through the warm darkness toward home. It was late when he slipped into the nearly darkened house, with only the hearth giving off light. Frank looked up from where he was mending some harness straps and said, "Where have you been? You missed Nonno's birthday dinner!"

Biaggio had completely forgotten, as time had seemed to stand still while in Marie Antonia's presence. Deep down he knew he should feel bad, but all he could think of was Marie. He would make it up to Nonno in the morning, giving him the present he bought at the market millinery and spending time with him.

The days passed slowly during that month and he was able only to slip away twice while in Cosenza. Once in the early evening when he saw Marie Antonia briefly with her family, and once when she went with the group of young people to visit some other relatives.

The last Sunday that Marie Antonia would be in Calabria, he left Bucita early in the morning for the cathedral in Cosenza. He knew his time was short and Marie Antonia would be leaving soon. He had to speak now or risk never seeing her again.

After the service he noticed that she was not with the others, so he looked around for her. She was sitting alone in the garden between the church and her cousin's home. Slipping into the garden quietly, he watched her as she gazed at the clouds floating in the western sky. He was on his knee beside her before she had the chance to react.

"Signorina Abbaté, I ... must speak to you. I know this is not proper. I know you are a lady and far above me," he pleaded in an honest, sincere tone.

Marie put out her hand to protest his words.

Not allowing himself to be silenced, he continued. "No, please let me finish." He knew he had to speak his mind, to state the words he had swirling around in his heart.

Again she raised her hand, her eyes wide and frightened and not a little sad.

"This cannot be, you must not speak!" she whispered, her words almost catching in her throat.

Restlessly, Biaggio kept pleading, "I must! I cannot be still!"

Marie shook her head and tried to explain, but the words would not come. He took her hand, her pale, delicate lady's hand, a hand that had not known work—wash water, dirt, tools, nothing. A hand so fine, so delicate. He knew he was beyond the rules now, but he couldn't stop himself.

"Signorina Abbaté, Marie Antonia, will you go with me to America? It will be a long, hard journey, and even after we get there, it won't be easy."

His words came out in a rush. He hadn't meant to say so much, but he was afraid—afraid of his feelings, afraid of her silence. His face was close to hers, his lips wanting so much to touch her fair cheek, his ears to hear her sweet, gentle voice say the words, the only words he ever wanted to hear. "Yes, yes, Biaggio, Biaggio."

But she shook her head slowly, sadly, as large teardrops rolled down her cheeks.

"Signorina ...."

"No, please! Call me by my name, Biaggio."

She shook her head more insistently, trying to pull her hand away.

"I know you care for me. I've seen it in your eyes since the first time I looked at you," he pleaded with her.

"I can't!" she finally blurted. "I am promised to another!" And she looked away over her shoulder.

Biaggio sat back on his heels, stunned into sudden silence. Of course this would be the way. One so lovely, so genteel, of such a fine family, would of course be promised, maybe even years ago when she was still a child. But she was also so strong, so self-willed. He had seen that, too! Wouldn't she ... couldn't she?

"But you don't want to ... don't have to ...."

"Biaggio," she whispered, and he was lost to her.

Suddenly he heard a distant voice, "Marie! Where are you hiding?"

Her cousins and friends came laughing into the churchyard. Biaggio leapt to his feet and stood back, out of the way, trying to regain his composure. Giorgio's father saw his face and then looked at Marie Antonia. He knew immediately what had happened. Taking Marie's arm and leading her into the house, he cast a disapproving glare down upon the young man.

Biaggio knew that all was lost. He stood still, his eyes seeing nothing until Giorgio came up, stood next to him, and broke the silence. "Come, Biaggio, we're having dinner."

"No, Giorgio, thank you, I must go. Thank your Mama and Papa for me. I must go."

"But Marie ...."

"Goodbye!" Biaggio called as he fled from the garden.

For days Biaggio walked around as one asleep. Never before had he given his heart away; never even thought of it. He had never even met anyone who had so much as warmed his heart, much less started this flame, this burning flame of pain! And never again would he allow anyone else do this to him!

His thoughts of going to America now became a consuming obsession. He had to do something with himself, had to have a task, a difficult, all-enveloping task, to set himself, to distract him, to forget her. He thought of nothing else than to make his way to America, the land of dreams and of fortune. There he would become one of her kind, would become good enough for a lady of her stature to marry. He would become rich and have money to throw around! He swore to himself, as he knelt on the cold, hard stone steps at the altar in the little church in Bucita: *I will make something of myself, of my family name. No one will look down upon me again like her uncle's pitying glare that day in the garden!*

Tears of pride and pain and frustration poured from his eyes. He looked up at the Blessed Virgin gazing down on him with her tender, loving eyes, and he heard her words again: "Go, Biaggio, go with my blessing." But the warmth he felt once again made the pain in his heart stronger, almost unbearable.

What did all of this mean? He didn't know and, possibly, he never would. All that his life was now good for was to make himself a better man, to make all the money he could, to improve himself, and to send money back to his family so they would not have to continue scraping such a hard living from the soil.

To America! The light burning in his eyes had taken on a desperate shine. In fact, his brothers and friends were sometimes a little afraid of him. The plans to leave soon became the only thing he would talk about. If before he rarely went to parties or dances, he no longer went at all.

"Francesco," Biaggio said to his brother, "we must go now, before all the other men of our country go. We must be among the first! We must get the best there is to offer!"

Frank conceded, "Yes, Biaggio, yes, all right, soon."

But Frank had his own concerns. He worried about the harvest, about their father's health, about the bad state of things in the village. There had been another dry summer, and crops were meager due to the drought.

They had lost Nonno the previous winter, when he had succumbed to an illness from the cold, damp chill of an unusually long season. On top of that, he had also had an accident in the fall that put his life in danger—a wheel broke on the wagon as he was driving along the edge of the steep path from the village. The side of the wagon fell off the road, and mule and man and wagon tumbled in a whirl of breaking wood and bones down the steep embankment. The mule broke two legs and had to be shot. Nonno only broke one, but the pain was so great he shouted for them to shoot him, too.

Peter had never been one to get overly excited about anything, and he watched quietly as his two older brothers lived their lives, each in his own way, but usually so alike, so in tune with each other. Now, however, he was surprised to see them almost disagreeing—about the burdens of the family, about its survival versus the unforeseen possibilities of America. Might Biaggio go to America without Frank? It was hard to imagine such a thing!

Almost in response to the drought, another flood came, but the soil was so dry that the land simply gave way when a sudden heavy summer storm blew in from the sea. Not unexpectedly, another epidemic closely followed, caused by the dampness and pestilence brought by the standing water left-over from the storm. Antonio's mama was one of the first in the village to fall ill—she had been ill the last time there had been such a sickness and had never really recovered. In a matter of days she was gone, and Antonio and his brothers and sisters wore stricken looks on their young faces.

Biaggio's sister Tomasina went about the village helping, as she always did, but one morning she was too weak to even rise from her bed. Fear clutched at Biaggio's heart as he knelt by her side, praying to God to protect her, to save her.

"I will do anything you ask, God. Please save my sister!"

Tomasina lay ill for the next two days, neither recovering nor growing worse. Biaggio prayed while he worked, while he ate, while he lay in bed, catching only fitful snatches of sleep. Finally, she slowly started getting her strength back.

Early the next morning, Papa led his two oldest sons down to the spring overlooking the wide valley between Bucita and Cosenza.

"My dear sons, it is time for you to help your family. You must go away from here, where life is so hard and getting harder. Go to this America, this land of promise. Save yourselves and your family name. Your sister wishes it, though in her heart she will grieve to see you go."

Papa paused to wipe a tear from his eye with his wrinkled, sun-weathered hand. He had aged so fast since Nonno passed, as if he were only holding on to this life to see that the family survived.

"I, too, will miss you, so very much. But this is right, it is needed. Go to safety, go to a place where you can do better than you will ever be able to do here."

Later that day their sister, who was resting easier, smiled at Biaggio and touched his hand as he knelt at her side. Biaggio had been coming to her each evening to read while she rested after dinner.

"You have stayed here with me, my dear brother, my Biaggio. You are a good brother. You should have a good life."

Then she closed her eyes and slept peacefully. The following day, she began her long journey to recovery.

Papa was still limping from his recent fall in the fields. It was an accident and the painful rehabilitation that followed took a toll. Being a man who had worked every day of his life since he could walk, it was difficult for him to sit, to be still

"It will not be easy to set sail for America, Biaggio," Papa sighed as he spoke, as always, slowly and carefully. "I am told it will be a long and dangerous trip to Napoli, and from there to the lands where our Italian tongue is not spoken. People in America do not understand our ways."

"Oh, Papa, I must go to America! Times here are poor, and the future only looks worse," Biaggio lamented. "My blood and sweat—and yours and Nonno's before—have been nourishing this soil for generations, and for what? We have nothing to show for our troubles!"

The old man coughed into his hand, then with his brown and gnarled fingers deftly pinched fragments of tobacco into a delicate cigarette paper, carefully rolling it and sealing it with a flick of his tongue. He settled uncomfortably on a wooden stool he had made with these same hands when they were still agile and useful.

"Yes, Biaggio, you must go as I've said before, but you must also remember your *famiglia*. Take your brother, Francesco, with you. You will need each other. You must stay together and protect one another, always. Leave young Pietro here for his sisters—for now, anyway."

Papa lit the cigarette, inhaled long and slowly, then sat up straight on his stool, squaring his shoulders as if he suddenly remembered who and where he was. He laid his hand on his son's shoulder and looked into his eyes.

"Yes, Biaggio, go with your brother to America. Go to save our family. Be blessed that there are two of you to remember our ways and what we have done for you here in Bucita."

Biaggio bowed his head to receive his Papa's benediction, his tears falling to the dry ground.

Papa pulled him close and hugged him tightly, whispering in his ear, "Don't tell your sisters, but I only wish I could go with you!"

"Biaggio, you and your brother are leaving for America tomorrow—I still cannot believe it! I don't understand how you could go after we've heard how they treat our people like dogs there!" Antonio stamped his foot in the dust and spun away from Biaggio, walking toward the road.

"I do not envy you at all!" Antonio shouted, turning back, his face flushed with emotion.

Biaggio just listened, waiting for his friend's anger to subside.

"They say that Italians can only find jobs in the ghetto ... or the factories at the lowest rates and the worst conditions! That a man cannot tolerate it! The stories you hear of fortunes are so few and far between! How many have gone from this wasteland of southern Italy, where there are no opportunities, only to find that America has the same poor existence! And then you're stuck there, with no family and no chance to come back!"

Biaggio walked to his friend and took his hand. It was true what Antonio had said: Some who had gone had returned with tales of the hard life in America, no better than here, but many more had stayed and succeeded.

"Antonio, you are my dearest friend. It is painful for me to leave you behind. But tomorrow I am going to America with my brother, as I have promised for so long. I can no longer stay in this unforgiving land with its unending chain of hardships. Look what it has done to you and your family."

Biaggio spoke with sadness, his eyes pleading with his friend to understand, to support him. He wanted to tell Tonio to come with them, but he knew it was impossible. He would never change his life or venture far from Bucita. Like most of the villagers, he had little chance for a better life. He now had to take care of his brothers and sisters until one day he would marry and start a family of his own. And the cycle would continue.

"It's true, Biaggio. This place took my papa and mama long before their time—but I cannot leave my homeland!" Antonio looked away from his friend's face, still unwilling to accept his leaving.

Biaggio turned to look at the rocky hills, dusty in the hot noonday sun.

"We barely make an existence from the soil, and our great-grandparents and their parents before them have died in the same villages and in the same poverty as generations before. I swore as a child I would break that chain! I will leave in the morning for a bright and prosperous future in America, you will see, Antonio! You will see that I, James Biaggio Bruno, will be a proud son of Bucita who will shine on these Calabrian hills that bore me and my family for generations! I am going to make it in America, you will see! Don't you forget that!"

Later, he stood alone thinking and watching the sun sink behind the rough stone hills. Of course, it is always hard for someone to leave behind loved ones and a homeland rich with family history. But he knew he must go. He felt the call to journey forward to this land of opportunity, to America. So many were leaving the sunny farmlands of Calabria for the dreams that they heard of, the dreams others told them. Dreams of that rich, distant land where there were fortunes to be made. Biaggio was determined to make his own fortune. And he believed his story would be told to his countrymen for years to come.

Chapter 2

A JOURNEY

The following morning in the spring of 1877, Biaggo and his brother Frank set off on foot to cross the Calabrian hills and countryside for Napoli where they would board a ship to America. Tomasina, Carmela, Papa and Peter watched as they disappeared over a hill and the distant farmland swallowed the two proud, young Bruno boys.

"Ah, Dear God, what choice do they have?" Papa asked, wiping the tears from his weathered cheeks.

"What choice do any of us have, when it comes to our future?" Tomasina answered. "So many young men who come from the southern lands of our Italian peninsula, lands that were once so fertile, are going off to America. Some of our villages will soon be made up of only old men and their women, or the sick, the uneducated ones who can't see the way out, or those who haven't the strength and courage to dream. Biaggio Bruno, my brother, was never such a man."

The two young men had little more than the shirts on their backs and the money for their passages. They had heard from a cousin of a person in a neighboring town that new immigrants to America were required to have twenty dollars to get into the country. But if they moved quickly after getting off the boat, they could slip into the city before being seen and avoid the processing on Garden Island.

Biaggio was grieving as they passed through and beyond Calabria. He thought of leaving his homeland, his family, his dear sisters, Peter, Papa. He thought of seeing this beautiful but treacherous country for the last time and a wave of melancholy passed over him. Even more, he grieved for the thing he refused to name, to think about or talk about—his love for the beautiful Marie Antonia.

His grief lessened somewhat as he walked along, looking at the beautiful landscape. In the spring of the year, the land was a lush green and the hills had the look of velvet. In the mornings, the mist was so thick that he and his brother could barely see the track ahead of them. But between the two of them, the sun above, and the sea often visible in the distance, they made their unerring way north to the port of Napoli and to the ship that would carry them away to a new life.

Finally, when one morning they reached the top of a ridge, the young men saw below a city so huge it spread from one end of the bay to well beyond the other end. They couldn't believe it. Napoli at last!

The view was worth a long rest on some great rocks almost the size of their village home. The brothers ate some of the bread with olive oil and the remaining prosciutto that Tomasina had tenderly packed. As they tore the bread and passed it back and forth, their conversation and mood changed. At first they had pointed out the wonderful buildings and points that interested them, some because of their size and others just because they were new to them. When they started to see the large ships on the shoreline at the port, they decided it was time to move on. They elected to go directly to the port and started down the steep sloping trail.

The two young men soon became engulfed in Naples itself. It was their first experience of such a city, the noises, the crowds, the streets that were a maze to them, filled with carts and people buying and selling. They could feel the energy and excitement of Napoli building in them as they made their way toward the port.

The docks were crowded, too, mostly with young men like themselves, a sack thrown over a shoulder holding all their possessions. Biaggio and Frank talked to others who were going to America, to South America, Brazil, Argentina.

"Maybe we should go to South America, Biaggio. It'd be warmer there because it's southern and they speak Spanish which is easier for us to understand," Frank said.

"No, I don't think so. It gets cold there, just like in North America, but at the opposite time. You remember when we studied geography, how it's winter in the north when it's summer in the south, and vice versa?"

"Uh, yes, of course, whatever you say. So, New York then, Biaggio?"

"Yes! New York, as planned."

The young men bought their tickets—twenty dollars each, more than they had ever paid for anything, more than they had ever even had at one time. They went to look for a place to eat and a place to sleep.

Men on the streets tried to sell them things—watches, fruit, jewelry, fancy trinkets.

"For your best girl!"

If Biaggio had not been annoyed by these men before, hearing that pushed him to the edge.

"Peddlers! Beggars! Thieves! All preying on innocent country folk who just want to improve their lot!"

"Gentlemen, come with me. I have a deal for you," offered a peddler with a somewhat dishonest smile.

The man had taken Biaggio by the elbow and tried to steer him away from the crowds to a more isolated place. He was dressed in a shiny suit that looked as if it had once been quite fine, perhaps on someone taller and thinner, and more than a few years ago.

"What do you want?" Biaggio asked roughly, pulling his arm out of the man's grasp.

"I can help you get jobs when you get to America. Just give me your tickets and your money and I will arrange everything for you."

Frank looked at his brother, raising his eyebrows in silent question just as he had done all their lives when they were in a pinch and needed to decide if they had to fight their way out or run. Biaggio nodded his head toward the wharf, his way of saying, "Not now, it's not worth soiling our hands." They turned and walked away from the man, Biaggio holding his tongue for fear of saying something that would get them into a fight after all.

"There's too much at stake here, now, or I would have beaten him and left him tied in his own cravat, deep in that dark alley he was trying to lead us to," Frank smiled in relief as they stepped back into the crowd.

"What kind of fools did he take us for?" Biaggio questioned, "I'd not be turning my life savings over to someone I've never met!"

Frank had turned back to see if the man was following them just in time to see that he had another potential victim, a country man in an ill-fitting suit who stood listening intently while a frightened-looking woman with a baby in her arms and two little ones clinging to her skirt stood watching.

"Biaggio, look, we have to help them," Frank said turning back.

Just then the peddler spun around and ran the other way, his victims looking after in complete surprise as a third man loped after the huckster with a club in his hand, shouting, "I told you to stay out of my territory!"

The incident was quickly forgotten as the air around them vibrated with the bellow of the horn from one of the big ocean liners rising like a mountain from a pier.

"Come, Biaggio, let's eat! I'm starved!"

"Wait," Biaggio said to his brother and turned back to the family who were huddled together, stunned by the noise and bustle of the street.

"Are you all right?" he asked the confused man.

The man looked a little embarrassed, then his wife murmured something to him and he nodded. Biaggio patted him on the shoulder and smiled, the whole family smiling with him. They were not Calabrians. Their dialect sounded as if they were from Campania, closer to Naples, but still a region of poor farmers.

"Be careful," Biaggio said to them, as slowly and clearly as he could, "and hide your money. Don't trust anyone."

The man nodded again and his wife clutched his arm, almost smiling.

Biaggio stopped suddenly on the dock, his foot inches from the gangplank that would carry him into his future. He looked, eyes wide, at the great ship that loomed like a huge city filling the horizon in front of him. He turned to look back at the mountains of Italy behind him, beyond the spires of Napoli, and thought about the great adventure ahead.

Frank had already gone aboard the great ocean liner, but Biaggio needed more time. He had been thinking about leaving Italy and going to America ever since he had been a schoolboy. Now that the time had come, he asked himself again, *Is it the right move?* Looking back toward the southern hills of his country, he was reminded of his youth. He thought of how, even as a fairly well-educated villager, he had been unable to go farther with his education because he was not a member of the privileged class. He did not even live in a city that offered opportunities for the kind of education that would help him rise out of the economically deprived village life that was his heritage. And because he was not of that privileged class, he would never have Marie Antonia, the girl that he loved, and now, on this day, he was leaving her behind forever, too.

Frank loved his village and his family—the thought of leaving them, perhaps forever, sent stabs of pain into his heart. He would miss passionately the evenings with relatives and friends, the long Sunday Masses in the village cathedral at San Fili, festivals with the splendid wines of his Calabria, and the gentle sounds of his native language. Papa was right, Biaggio was glad to be boarding this ship with his brother, for now Frank was all he had of home.

"Biaggio, come look!" shouted Frank, leaning over the rail of the great ship and waving to his brother. The ship was new and beautiful, white and shining in the sun.

"What is it?" Biaggio asked, as he walked carefully up the gangway to the inside passage of the huge ship.

"Our bunks! You won't believe them!" Frank exclaimed. "We have never had it so fine before!" he said with excitement as he showed him their accommodations.

As he answered his brother, Biaggio thought of the dusty little villa in Bucita where they had grown up. "We must get used to our new life and what life in America will bring to us. We are not going to be defeated! The blood that we share—our strong, red Italian blood—will help us build a prosperous future in our new homeland. We are on our way!"

The two young brothers were a team, a family. Now more than ever, they had to work together toward a bright and better future.

On second glance, the brothers' quarters were clean and neat, but small and close, and poorly lit. As they waited, more and more people were led into steerage; men on one side, women and children on the other, husbands and wives separated, children crying at the top of their lungs and running wildly in the narrow corridors. Very soon all the beds were taken and people were told to find a space on the floor—the deck, the rude sailors called it. One had to step over the belongings of other travelers to go anywhere on the ship.

At first, Biaggio was glad they had arrived early enough to get bunks, but he began to doubt whether he could survive in this crowded space for two weeks—fourteen long days! He thought about just going to the outside deck, finding a space there, maybe in a lifeboat, to spend the voyage. Biaggio loved to roam, loved his freedom—how would he ever last two weeks? All these strangers, foreigners, some from other areas, regions and provinces that were enemies of his people such as those from the regions of the Piedmont or Lombardia.

Frank saw the growing panic in his brother's face. He smiled, took his arm, and said,

"Come, Biaggio, tell me some of your stories of how it will be in America! Here we are, grown men, who've lived more than twenty years in the same small space of the world, a tiny space compared to how big this earth is, and in two weeks—only two weeks—we will be on the other side of that earth, in a completely different country! Two weeks! It's a miracle! By the Blessed Virgin, a miracle!"

So the brothers spent as much time as possible on the deck in the fresh air, only going to their bunks to sleep late at night, sometimes having to roust someone who had taken advantage of their absence. The area that had been beautiful and clean and neat on that first day was very soon messy, then dirty, then filthy, then disgusting. With so few workers to clean, so little water to clean with, and little incentive to do so in the first place, the area never improved. The passengers did all they could, but they, too, were hampered by the overcrowded space.

As Biaggio lay in his bunk gazing at the ceiling inches from his face, or on the outside deck gazing at the sky or stars, he could see only his vision of America or his vision of Marie Antonia. Heaven and hell, hell and heaven, so mixed together in his mind that he began to fear he was losing awareness. Sometimes a melancholy would descend on him. He would sit up abruptly, more than once cracking his skull on the ceiling above the bunk and waking others in the confined space. Frank would talk quietly to him, "Peace, brother, we're almost there."

As he lay sleepless on the open deck, gazing at the stars, Biaggio thought, *I must plan how I will look for work. I must get a good job, not one of those horrible jobs that wear a man to his death. I must hold my head high and show them that I am worth more than that! They must pay me a decent wage and not try to make me do hard, back-breaking work. I must have work that my family can respect, that is good for the family name.* Then, more often than not, he fell into a fitful slumber.

In spite of the conditions on the ship, the days passed faster than the brothers had imagined. They met many people, learned many things. The ship stopped in Liverpool, and more people were crammed in, including a couple of Irishmen, one with a deck of cards in his coat pocket.

"A game of chance, gentlemen?" the taller of the two asked.

Though the man spoke English, of which Frank and Biaggio knew only a smattering, the deck of cards was quite familiar.

Biaggio, curious, nodded his head. Frank, the cautious one, shook his head and touched his brother's arm.

Biaggio smiled at him, as if to say, "Don't worry. I won't lose all my money. I've waited too long for this and want it too much to ruin it now."

Apparently the Irishmen had already been to America and had made some Italian friends, so they were somewhat familiar with Italian, enough, at any rate, to communicate with the brothers. Despite the language barrier, the men found some others for a game and soon the bets were flying. A couple of men were losing heavily but showed no signs of quitting. Biaggio was winning a little more every couple of hands, but not as much as the two Irishmen.

Then the dinner bell rang and the game broke up. Biaggio and Frank sat on the deck next to the two newcomers. As the men ate together, they talked about their arrival in their new country, quickly overcoming any communication problems.

"The smartest thing to do is cut and run as soon as we land," one of the Irishmen recommended.

"Yes, we heard that. Someone sent home a letter telling the rest of us what to do," Frank commented. "There will be a lot of confusion when we land at Garden Island. What with all the baggage and people speaking different languages and children running about, everything will be out of control. We dock right in the city, and it's not too difficult just to melt into the confused crowds, at the right time."

As they talked about their plans, the four men realized they had a lot in common even though they were from very different countries.

"I'm Jack Kelly from County Clare in Ireland, and this is Patrick Ayres. He's a quiet one, but the brains of this team. I'd been dead afore now, weren't for 'im."

Ayres smiled a slow, shy smile, and nodded at Kelly. Biaggio thought they seemed a lot like brothers, like Frank and himself, and felt it was a gift from God for the four of them to have met. They exchanged information about themselves, about their homelands, their families, their hopes and dreams for the future.

"You have been to America before?" Biaggio asked the Irishmen.

Kelly replied, "Yes, we sailed two years ago for the first time. We went back home last month—to Ireland, that is—to do some work for our employers."

He grinned at that, and James and Frank glanced at each other, sensing that this was some secret that they would need to know and would find out if they paid attention and stuck close to this clever man. It was clear that Kelly and Ayres fully intended to become something in this new country, just as Biaggio and Frank did.

From then on the four men met to share their meals, and toward the end of the trip, Jack said,

"Let's keep in touch. I think we have the same goals and we can help one another." The others nodded in agreement and they shook hands all around.

Finally the trip was coming to an end. Biaggio stood proudly at the rail of the ship, watching as land approached. He thought about the amazing events he had lived through in the short time since he had left his home. More had happened to him in less than a month than had occurred in the whole rest of his life. Many thoughts raced through his mind. In later years when he would recount the tale of their journey across the ocean to America, he would say,

"That day, for the first time, we could see the great city of New York in the distance. It looked like mountains at first, but as we drew closer we could see that what we had thought were rocks were actually buildings! So tall, and so many! And there were so many ships in the port I wondered how ours could even get to the dock.

"Manhattan was the area of New York City where we went ashore. We needed to find a place to stay and get settled temporarily. Then immediately we would look for work.

"And now, to our new homeland!"

At last the ship docked. The gangplanks were lowered, and the mass of passengers picked up their belongings and began inching toward their new home. Working together with Kelly and Ayres, the Bruno brothers watched for their chance to slip through the crowd. Suddenly, they were in the street, going as fast as they could walk while being careful not to look suspicious. Quickly they melted into the bowels of the big city, New York City.

When they finally stopped to catch their breaths, Kelly slapped each of them on the back.

"Well done, men!"

"Yes! Thanks to you!" Frank said. He had had a close call when he slipped as he stepped off the crowded gangway. Then when he reached the sturdy stationary wooden floor of the dock he had lost his footing. Balancing was difficult after being at sea so long.

When they finally stopped, Biaggio laughed out loud, then leaned his head back and threw his arms in the air, shouting out, "We're here! We made it!" It was almost unbelievable.

"Yes!" Frank responded heartily. "We're Americans now."

CHAPTER 3

FINDING A WAY

On one street is Germany and all the s*chnitzel* one can eat; on another street is Poland with *kielbasa* and *pierogis*. Next, one can sample French pastries or English scones or Irish stew or even Chinese duck! It's like being able to walk around the world! Biaggio loved looking and sniffing the varied aromas in the air, but he always came back to Little Italy, to the smell of garlic and pasta and Italian tomato sauce—the aromas that brought him back to his senses.

The tiny confined quarters in the ship turned out to be merely a taste of what was to come for Biaggio and Frank. At first, the room that they were able to afford was worse than they could ever have imagined—tiny, dark cramped, and overrun with vermin. They even had to share the space with half a dozen other new immigrants.

In spite of his excitement at being in New York City, a part of Biaggio remained sad—the part of him that loved Marie Antonia. While his arrival in America had served to somewhat awaken him from his melancholy, the desperate accommodations only fanned the flames of his desire to rise, to get rich, and to show the whole world as well as Marie Antonia, that he was James Biaggio Bruno and he was somebody. He also decided the time had come for him to go by his English name, James, so that he could fit in to this new world.

"We'll find you some work and get you out of here, don't worry," Jack Kelly told the brothers. "There's plenty of work for men with your ambition and strength."

Soon, with Kelly's help, the brothers found day jobs in construction, a church here, a bank there, sometimes with Irishmen, sometimes with Italians. They were always on the lookout for fellow Calabrians, but so far had not met any.

Frank and James visited with Kelly and Ayres whenever they had the chance. The brothers were working hard to learn English and their new Irish friends helped them as much as they could.

Their first steady employment came about by chance. Frank was walking along the edge of Little Italy on Spring Street, heading back to the flat, when an older man walking in front of him dropped his packages. Fruits and vegetables and bread rolled all over the street. Frank sprang to help, gathering up the food and offering to carry the parcels. The man's face suddenly lit up with genuine delight.

"*Si*, I came from Reggio di Calabria, about thirty years ago." The two men could not shake hands right away as Frank's were full of the older man's packages. But he patted Frank on the shoulder and said,

"Thank you. Please carry my groceries for me and be my guest at supper."

Frank and his new friend started on their way. He was so delighted to finally find a countryman that he forgot all about getting back to his brother.

"Yes, of course, thank you. *Ringraziamenti!*"

Senor Alberti told Frank that he had immigrated many years earlier, before so many fellow Italians had started to come. He, too, had been a poor young man when he left, but he had started a successful business in New York and was quite comfortable now in his old age. His problem, was that he had no sons, no daughters' husbands, and no grandchildren to carry on his business.

"My daughter, she is old now, she is childless. My son, oh, my dear son, died when he was just starting to be a man. So sad. He was working for me when another man from a Sicilian family decided to move into my territory. He trapped my son in a car and drove it into the East River just over there." Senor Alberti pointed to a point in the river. Frank touched the man's hand respectfully, sympathizing with his loss, but not quite understanding the story.

Senor Alberti asked Frank about himself and Frank told him about his family, about James, and how they were working at odd jobs, hoping to find something permanent.

The older man saw in Frank the same youthful ambitions he had had so many years earlier. The test of time had only encouraged the man to work harder for his success. Now that he was older and successful, he needed younger blood to keep the business from stagnating. He seized upon Frank's Calabrian heritage, hoping to find out if he was the young man he appeared to be. He was not worried about Frank's honesty or his confidence. Calabrese men usually trusted one another automatically as part of their culture. The area they come from is so small and isolated that their strong family ties extend to the community. Everyone helps everyone else because they know someone related to that someone else. No one ever spoke to outsiders about confidential topics. The community is a part of the larger family, a family to be trusted.

Frank felt the warmth of his village in the man's speech. He felt as if he had found a long lost uncle. The two men talked for hours. They covered topics related to the old country, the new city that they were working so hard to be a part of, and the opportunity that was available to Frank and his brother. The whole meeting was so exciting that Frank forgot the time. Suddenly he said, "I should have been home hours ago! My brother will be so worried!"

"Go now," said Senor Alberti. "Then let us meet again tomorrow."

"Yes, let's," answered Frank, nodding his head. "I'll bring James with me."

Frank practically ran the entire way back to their room. He was excited and certain that they would all be in agreement. He felt the chance meeting could turn into an excellent opportunity for all three of them.

That evening the brothers talked about the meeting and the opportunity that had presented itself. Frank told James that Senor Alberti wanted both of them to join his import company in positions of leadership. Alberti was delighted with their excellent grasp of English. He felt they would rise through the ranks as their knowledge of the business increased and their experience showed where they would work best.

James had just stepped out of a small bakery with the loaves of bread the brothers would use for their lunches the next day when a tall young man sprinted past him with a stocky older man in close pursuit. No fool, James stepped back into the doorway until they passed, then leaned out to see what would transpire. Very soon the older man overtook the younger and proceeded to smash him against the brick wall of the building a few doors down.

"I told you last time, you have one chance only to make your payment. Then it's too late."

"No, Luigi, no, please! I'll get it, I promise. My sister, she gets a ..."

"Your sister, huh? You give me your sister for what you owe me, huh?"

"No! I give you money for what I owe you!"

"Not soon enough you didn't."

The stocky man held the other man's throat and beat his head against the wall until his blood poured down the wall and onto the sidewalk.

"Hey, Luigi, you no get your money that a-way, do you?" The owner of the pool hall on the other side leaned in his doorway observing the beating in much the same way he would as if he had been watching a game of billiards inside his hall.

"From the next one, I do. This one's an example. Don't mess with Luigi."

"Ah, yeah, an example."

James had just decided it was time to move on when Luigi dropped his victim and turned to face James.

"You like this, huh?"

James said nothing.

"You a friend of his?"

"No, sir. I'm a friend of yours."

Luigi laughed at that, showing several gaps in his front teeth.

"I like that. I like you. I like your looks. You want a job?"

"Ah, last week I would have, but I got a job with my uncle now."

Luigi nodded, the common bond of family understood, the respected hint of a lie acknowledged and accepted due to James's confident tone.

"Listen, you need anything, you come to me, okay?" James nodded at the suggestion.

"*Ringraziamenti.* How do I find you?" he asked.

"Just look around," the stocky man said. James nodded again.

James and Frank soon moved away from the rat-infested tenement where they had spent their first few nights. They had moved twice since then, each time to a better, bigger, cleaner, and of course, more expensive, place.

James did look around and began to see Luigi or Luigi's men everywhere, every card game, every whorehouse, every pool hall. James liked to play cards, he liked to win, but not enough that he lost his head. He could tell when he was going to have a bad night and leave, but he never left without making sure that Luigi got a tip. James made sure Luigi knew he respected him.

What James liked even more, however, was the thought of being in charge of a card game, or a pool hall, or a house of ill repute. He wanted to learn everything he could from Luigi.

Soon Luigi entrusted James with small jobs, collecting from a reluctant client, carrying a small package to another borough in the big city, perhaps watching someone's house for a few nights, or paying off a policeman for turning his head after a fight. In a short time, James had his own turf, his own work. He was still going to his daily job, mostly for cover and to keep his hand in. But he worked the hours convenient to him, and his boss, Senor Alberti, knew better than to complain. The money that he was making working for Luigi made the pay from his day job seem insignificant.

One day, the brothers received a letter postmarked Bucita. The letter was from their sister Tomasina—Papa had died. James and Frank were deeply saddened. They had known their father's health was failing because of the fall he had before they left Italy. But they never realized that he was so ill. The news was especially hard to take because they were not in their village with their family. They were so disheartened because their family could not be together in their sorrow.

Soon after, James and Frank met up again with their friends Kelly and Ayres to talk about some things they could do to move up faster in the new world. Together the men spent hours imagining the possibilities. They drank the red wine of Italy and smoked big Cuban cigars until deep into the night, indifferent to the fact that they had to get up early the next morning. This was the important part of life, the talking, the planning and the camaraderie. Anyone could go to work each day; what these men were searching for was how they could be different, how they could rise above the common folk.

James had been wondering how a new man could move up in the business in this big city with so many huge, powerful families already working there. He didn't want to stay at the bottom, be a little fish for some other not much bigger fish for the rest of his life. James wanted to be the boss.

They talked about perhaps moving to a smaller city, away from New York, and starting a business there. They thought about the small towns north of the city, discussed what businesses, what industries there were in the outlying areas that a man could succeed in, could use to rise to power.

Kelly had been working for the railroad, heading a construction crew laying new track. He had heard that some of the railroad construction crews were laying track to the mines in nearby eastern Pennsylvania. Laying the track right to the mine entrance was the best way to transport coal, he was told. He said he had also heard some of the men on the railroad talking about how the mine bosses needed more and more workers.

The mine bosses would send men back to their homeland to contract with men who were seeking jobs in the new world, men who wanted to come to America. The bosses would help those men pay their passage to America and the mine employees who enlisted them would receive a small fee for their services.

"We've been doing this for the railroad," Kelly explained, nodding toward his friend. "That's why we went back to Ireland; why we were on the boat you were on."

James and Frank looked at each other and James grinned. They knew there were plenty of men in Calabria who would give their right arms to come to America, would jump on the next boat if they had a little help. James had gotten a letter from Antonio just the week before with tales of political unrest, more disease, a drought, possible famine.

Yes, men were available in Calabria, and James and Frank could help. Furthermore, the mining companies were willing to go to great lengths to build tracks to their new mine shafts, willing indeed, to pay bribes to whomever could help them.

James fell back in his chair with a big grin on his face. This conversation was sounding more and more like a way they could succeed in their new country. Finally, some of what they had heard about the Promised Land was coming to light!

Patrick then added that they also knew some Irish people who had settled in the mountains of eastern Pennsylvania, friends of theirs from their home county in Ireland. He said that he and Jack had been thinking of moving there themselves to be nearer to those people, the closest they had to family in the America.

A seed had been planted: the idea of moving west to a small town in Pennsylvania and beginning work there. That seed began to grow quickly and take shape in the minds of James and Frank Bruno.

In addition to learning from Luigi, James was learning from another teacher. Dominic was a grocer in his day job, but everyone knew his real job was precinct captain. He lived in the building next to James and Frank.

The position of precinct captain was one of the lower levels of an intricate and rigid hierarchy that formed the Tammany system, the true governing body of New York City at the time. James had been studying the system and followed its process carefully, though from a respectful distance. James was fascinated by politics—he had begun to see that as the real way to get ahead and to acquire power, lots of power.

After they had started to work for Senor Alberti, James and Frank began studying English in greater depth, as well as learning to read and write. Though they were doing well working at Senor Alberti's company and still earning money on the side working with Luigi, gambling as well as watching the moves of the politicians, none of it was happening fast enough for James.

Senor Alberti seemed to be coming back to life since the young men from his home province had arrived, catching some of their youthful enthusiasm and even appearing younger. James was happy to see that, but he also realized that if he and Frank stayed with their new mentor, there would be nowhere for them to go, nowhere for them to move up for a long time.

Through his contacts with Luigi, James had met some young people who liked to dance and listen to music in the halls in town and wear fashionable clothes and shoes. He took note of the way they dressed, found out where they got their clothes, and soon he had attired himself and Frank like men-about-town.

The brothers bided their time. Patrick had gone ahead to a small village in northeastern Pennsylvania close to Hazelton. He had been able to transfer his job with the railroad, as the lines in Pennsylvania were expanding toward the mining areas and laborers were in demand. Patrick also obtained a supervisory position at Lehigh and Wilkes-Barre Coal Company. Patrick liked the area and was soon sending back letters full of enthusiasm.

One day in early October, Jack Kelly suggested that he, James and Frank take a short train trip to Pennsylvania to visit Patrick. The brothers agreed. They were beginning to feel it was time to make a move to the country to the west, time to start taking advantage of their options.

The three men sat on the train as it rolled slowly out of the dirty, smoky city which seemed to go on forever. Eventually city streets gave way to farmlands, to woods and rivers, then hills which grew steeper, tree-covered, and finally, full-fledged mountains.

James sat silently gazing out the window, oblivious of the other men, who sat drinking wine, smoking cigars, and discussing the upcoming election. He felt a peace come over him such as he had not felt since they had left Bucita. Then he understood. This country reminded him of his home in Calabria. He could almost see the green mountains there; not quite as high as here, but more than that, the land was wild and free! So much better than the city.

The men talked about the work available in the mountains—railroad construction, mining, securing workers for the mines, and the many support businesses needed in a remote town. They slept that night out in the open, lulled to sleep by the crickets and the wind in the trees.

James woke early, feeling completely refreshed. The early morning sun shone in pale beams through the thick trees, reminding him of that morning in the cathedral, so long ago it seemed like another lifetime. He thought of Marie, of her lovely young face, her shining red-gold hair, her spark, and he felt peace in his heart. This place was like a balm to his soul, and the pain, the melancholy, which had been so deep in him had finally gone. He could now think of Marie without falling apart. He was so excited about his new life in America, especially the changes still to come, that he could clearly see how he could carry on. Once and for all, James felt free.

The friends hiked around the rest of the day exploring the small mining towns. At dusk, they boarded the train back to New York City and discussed the merits of the area they had visited. James talked with animation of the possibilities of one of the mining towns, both business-wise and politically, and he sang the praises of the beautiful countryside.

"I think this is it, this will be our place in this country," he said to Frank and Jack. "I feel some powerful sense of destiny, that we've been led here, by you, by the railroad, by the mines.

"I think that the mining district of Kline Township is the pot of gold at the end of the rainbow for us."

The two men nodded and Frank spoke, "Yes, I agree with James. This place seems ideal in so many ways, plenty of potential. I'm ready to start tomorrow!"

The men laughed together and ordered another round of beer. All too soon they were rolling through the streets of the city, crowded, clamoring, and brightly lit though it was not yet sunrise. They toasted each other and their fledgling enterprise, then bade each other farewell at the station, making plans to meet again the following Sunday.

When James returned to the flat the next day, he found a letter from Calabria.

> Dear James,
>
> I hope this letter finds you well. All is well here with my family. My wife and I have a new baby son who is healthy and strong, especially in his lungs. My sister Sylvia is planning to be married next spring.
>
> The weather has been very dry this summer, almost a drought. We're not sure if this is better or worse than the floods. My cousin, Marie Antonia, whom you met, has had tragedy in her life. Her husband, Franco Coscarello, died of typhoid, though she and her young son Francis were never sick. Her father was also ill but is now recovering.
>
> Please write again. I enjoyed your last letter and look forward to hearing more about your life in America.
>
> Your friend,
>
> Giorgio

James sat down hard on the steps of the building, the breath knocked out of him. Marie was free! At last, she was free. He thought of his feelings on the day before and was amazed at the sudden changes in his world. He carefully folded the letter and slipped it into his breast pocket and turned to walk up the street. Frank was working late that night, so James walked and walked all on his own, thinking over his situation.

Sorting out his feelings was difficult for James. Just the day before he had given up, had thought that chapter of his life was closed. But now! He realized that he still loved Marie, but he had been afraid to open his heart again to that possibility because of the pain he always felt. He finally walked home and found Frank at the table, eating his dinner and reading the paper. James handed him the letter.

Frank looked up at James and said, "You still love her, don't you?" then smiled as the look on James's face answered his question.

"Go to her! She's free now! She loved you then but went along with what her family wanted. Write to Giorgio and ask him to help you!"

The brothers talked it over again and finally James decided to write Giorgio asking if it would be proper for him to visit Marie. They both felt that the reason Giorgio had written the letter was to tell James of Marie Antonia's situation and to leave the door open for his return. Giorgio knew of the flame between the two. He had seen it in their shy faces every time they were together, but never spoke of it for that would have been improper since she was engaged at the time. But now, her father would be open to a new husband to care for his daughter as she was a newly widowed young woman with a child.

A few weeks later Frank obtained employment with a Lehigh Valley Railroad construction crew and gave his notice to Signor Alberti. It was not an easy task, as Signor Alberti was now like a father to the brothers. Frank was delighted when Alberti told him he knew that the time had come for them to move on.

He was glad to see that while the time had arrived quickly for them, it was too soon for him. But he did not hesitate to say, "Go and be prosperous. Anything you need just ask me, my 'sons.'"

Within a week, Frank began working and boarding with Kelly and Ayres in the little mining town of Bunker Hill in eastern Pennsylvania. His job was to help the planning and surveying crew as they decided the best way to get tracks to the mines. His skill, determination, and cleverness helped him rise quickly.

Within months he was helping make decisions about where the track should be laid, and not long afterward he became the supervisor of the crew.

The length of time it took for a letter to cross the ocean could vary wildly, but it could never be less than the time it took a ship to go back and forth. Then add the time needed for a letter to get from the ship across the land to the recipient, for the recipient to read it, ponder it, decide whether or not to respond, then to write and send a response. To James the stretch of time seemed almost as long as the rest of his life.

But James had little time to sit around and wait. He was anxious to get started working for the mine in Pennsylvania. So, one fine Monday morning, dressed in a proper suit and wearing a fedora on his head and looking entirely the proud peacock, James stepped into the offices of Honey Brook Colliery.

"How do you do, sir?" he asked the Honey Brook Colliery supervisor on that cool September morning.

The supervisor replied cordially, "Things are a looking up these days. My name is Johnny Marco, sir, and you are ...?"

"I am James Bruno. I am from Cosenza, in Calabria, Italy. I understand that you have need of laborers for your colliery, and I have come here today to offer to obtain those laborers for you." James had no intention of starting as a laborer himself.

James had an ostentatious manner, but his charm and tone of respect always won the day. Throughout his entire life James used his eloquent speech to persuade others to do his will as well as reveal his determination and drive for great things to come.

His foray into the mining industry was the first of several steps in his climb up the ladder of success and of the Bruno family's making their mark on a small town in eastern Pennsylvania.

Mr. Marco, for his part, recognized a man who could and would do what he promised. Within a very short time, James was offered the position of colliery supervisor and began preparations to supply the mine with laborers from Italy.

James traveled back to New York City to begin settling his affairs. He took time to say a fond farewell to Signor Alberti.

James and Frank had met a couple of young men from Calabria who would take their places in Aberti's import company, and they promised Signor Alberti that they would stay in contact with him. James knew there would always be uses for an import company, and he fully intended to employ the services of Signor Alberti in the future.

James also spoke at length with Luigi about starting card games in Pennsylvania. Luigi offered him pointers, told him what to look for in employees, and gave him some treasured secrets of the trade. He even gave him one of his lieutenants, a man whose new bride wanted to move out of the city.

James paid his respects to Dominic as well. Dominic was fighting to become ward boss. Even though he had seniority and was more than qualified, he was being passed over because he was not Irish. Dominic told James to come back to visit and told him that anytime he wanted political advice, he had only to call.

James hated to discontinue his English studies but he was determined to get some classes started in Bunker Hill as soon as he was settled. James spent his last nights in the city socializing with his friends and saying his farewells. But even with all such activity, his mind was always calculating where a letter might be in passage to and from Italy.

When James returned to the flat the next day, he found a letter from Calabria.

When Giorgio's letter arrived James realzed that he already knew what it would say.

> Dear James,
> Yes, of course, come and we will go together to
> see Marie Antonia. She remembers you and will
> be happy to see you again. The marriage did
> not last long but it was her duty to her family.
> I always believed her heart went with you. Of
> course she is still in mourning, but by the time
> you can arrange passage here she will be able
> to attend to visitors again. Let me know your
> plans.
>
> Fondly,
> Giorgio

James now had two reasons to return to Italy—to claim the woman he loved and to begin the process of importing workers for the mine. The construction crew that Frank supervised would soon be unable to work because of the cold and snows of winter, so together the brothers made plans to return to their homeland. It took them some time to make their preparations. As it was late in the year for an Atlantic crossing, they traveled south to catch one of the last ships sailing before winter set in.

When the brothers reached Napoli, Giorgio met them at the docks. Frank went overland to Bucita to start looking for laborers.

One of the many lessons the two young men had learned during their time in New York City was how to bring their fellow countrymen to work in the United States. After locating several suitable men, they would pay their passage on a ship, meet them when they arrived in America, and take them to their prearranged place of work. The brothers would then give the new workers the opportunity to rent a place to live from them and they would keep a part of the workers' wages until all the money was repaid. In other words, the new workers were charged a fee for getting them a job, telling them what to do when they arrived, what to say to the officials and for finding them a new life.

And James and Giorgio found passage to Agrigento, Sicily, where James would propose to Marie Antonia.

When the two men arrived at Marie Antonia's house, the maid showed James and Giorgio into a small but elegant drawing room and asked them to be seated while she went to tell her mistress they had arrived. Giorgio chatted for a moment but James was too nervous to talk, and soon Giorgio gave up and studied the pictures lining the sideboard. James had to force himself to remain seated, his desire to pace barely restrained.

Suddenly Marie Antonia was there, framed in the doorway, her soft fair hair hidden under a black lace mantilla, her slim figure shrouded in black silk. Although the required period of mourning was long past, it was customary to continue to wear the mourning shroud in public.

James stood and gazed at her, waiting for her to speak, his hand wanting to reach for hers.

"Biaggio ...."

Finally, after all that time, all those miles, all that waiting, she said what he had always wanted to hear—his name on her lips.

"Marie Antonia," James spoke to her in a low voice. Crossing the room in a few steps, he took her hand and kissed it as he had seen his elegant friends in the city do.

Giorgio smiled at this suave young man, who had been so tongue-tied the first time he had met Marie. Then he slipped out the side door leaving the two alone.

A shadow falling across her face brought Marie Antonia back to the world.

"Oh, look how late it is! Come, supper should be ready. Now where did Giorgio disappear to?"

She took James's hand so naturally that he smiled. She looked up and blushed, realizing what she had done, but he held tight to her hand, then brought it once again to his lips.

"I'm not going to let you go again, Marie Antonia, never again!"

She smiled, and looked at their hands clasped, then back up into his eyes.

"Don't worry, Biaggio, I won't go away from you ever again!"

"Mama, what are you saying?"

"I am saying that he is not a person with whom one such as you may associate."

Marie shook her head slowly back and forth as if to clear the fog from her mind.

"He's a fine man. He's quite successful in America. I don't understand what you think is wrong."

"We know how young men who go to America make their money. He was a *paesano* when he left and he still is—no fancy clothes can change that!"

"Mama, do you have any idea how arrogant you sound? I am a grown woman with a life and a mind of my own. I did as you told me once, and married for you, and now I shall do as I want. I have promised James I will marry him and I shall!"

"You shall not! I forbid it! Marie Antonia, you look at me when I am speaking to you! Where do you think you are going?"

"I am going to be with my future husband."

"You will do no ..."

"If you will not accept him then you will lose me, too. Is that what you want, Mama?"

"You ungrateful child!" her mother cried.

"You have Papa and your sons. You do not need me here, I must do as my heart tells me." Then, after a long pause Marie Antonia reluctantly added a sorrowful, "Goodbye, Mama."

James was not shocked by Marie Antonia's mother's reaction to him, but he was upset that Marie Antonia had to choose between love and family.

"Marie, my love, I don't want to make this much trouble for you, for your family!"

"Biaggio, you are my family now, yes?"

"Yes, yes, of course, I will take you home, but I'm so deeply sorry your mother feels this way!"

"Yes, so am I, but there's nothing to be done. She's as stubborn as I am. I can only hope that someday she will reconsider, when ..." she looked up at James, shyly for her, and continued, "...when you and I have babies, her grandchildren."

He smiled and pulled her close to him, touching her smooth cheek with his lips.

"Marie, my sweet Marie ...."

"I want a new life for myself, I want to go with you to America, to get away from this old, sick country. I want a new life for my son, for my children, for our children!"

She stopped for a moment, looking across the street at the house of her childhood, then continued, "You told me those long years ago that it would be a long hard journey, and even after we get there it wouldn't be easy. It isn't easy here! At least there I will be with you. Yes, Biaggio, I will go with you to America.

My children will be pioneers." She laughed, but at the same time James could see the passion in her eyes. She shared his deep desire to have the best that life could offer them.

James grabbed Marie Antonia's hand and spun her around in a wild dance: so happy that she would go with him. After those long, painful years when he thought he had lost her, he knew now she shared his enthusiasm. Now she was his. Marie would go with him to the land of his dreams, their dreams. Ah, sweet Mother of God, she was his!

Together with Giorgio, Marie Antonia and James left Sicily and sailed back to the mainland, to the village of Bucita. It was a long trip across mountainous central Sicily to the coast at Messina. Once there they had to stay the night so that in the early morning they could buy tickets for passage on the ferry to Reggio Calabria at the toe of Italy.

Eventually the three friends got to Cosenza where they left the train and headed up the mountains to tiny Bucita. Marie Antonia chose not to go to Giorgio's home in Cosenza, so as not to put her aunt in an uncomfortable position. James's friend Antonio offered to let her stay with his family until she and James could be married.

While James had been in Agrigento, Frank had been hard at work asking around the area for men who wanted to go to America. In addition, what he had found was a dancing partner from the old days. Josephine was a bit older than he, but had married late and had always had a fondness for younger men, Frank in particular. Like Marie Antonia, she had lost her husband; but unlike Marie Antonia, she had no children.

Josephine listened eagerly to Frank's descriptions of life in the United States, while feeding him sumptuous treats of apricots and honey. Later she started suggesting to him names of young men who might want to go to America.

Not too long after, James and Frank made their vows to the women they loved in a single wedding ceremony attended by nearly everyone in their village. The two newly married couples took a short trip around the southern tip of Italy, visiting family and friends in San Fili, Cosenza and small villages in Calabria.

As they traveled, they continued to collect names of men who wanted to emigrate. While they were in Reggio di Calabria, they paid a visit to Signor Alberti's family, giving them letters and gifts he had sent.

In the late winter, James and Frank began preparations to return to America, promising their brides they would return the following year to take them to their new homes. Such was a normal pattern for families immigrating to the New World. The two wives promised that they would do their part to fill those homes as both were expecting babies at the end of the year.

"I will find you a fine home in the beautiful mountains of Pennsylvania, a home suitable for you, my beautiful Marie Antonia," James said to Marie.

"I don't need a fine home," Marie replied. "Any home will do as long as it's with you."

"I hate to leave you so soon after finding you again!"

"Yes, it's too soon for me also, but the time will fly and we'll be together again!"

The journey back to America and Pennsylvania was uneventful for James and Frank, but the time without their wives was intolerable. The brothers worked hard, as always, saved their money, and planned their new homes. After many months, a letter finally arrived from Marie Antonia: their son was born and all was well.

> My darling Marie Antonia,
>
> I am so proud to be a papa! With you, my beloved, as his mama.
>
> Yes, I have thought much about his name. I want my son to be a leader, a conqueror! I want him named for Guiseppe Garibaldi!
>
> It cannot be soon enough that I see you again, and my son for the first time, and little Francis too. Francis is your son, but now he is mine as well, we are a family.

May the spring come quickly!

Your loving husband,
James

Marie read the letter aloud to James's family. Tomasina said, "Ah, Biaggio, still playing the soldier!"

She smiled at Marie who gazed lovingly at the sleeping baby in her arms.

"He should have his mother's name," Tomasina said gently, not wanting to antagonize this strong-willed young woman. Marie conceded and wrote back to her husband,

> We must name our son Guiseppe Maria here in Italy, but when we get to America let us call him Guiseppe Giacomo—Joseph James.
>
> Marie

James read Marie's letter and nodded. Yes, that was right, in both countries. He wrote back immediately.

> Yes! Guiseppe for our heroes, for Guiseppe Garibaldi, for Guiseppe Mazzini, Joseph. Maria for his Mama and James for his papa who will take him to America. Guiseppe Maria, Joseph James, the hero, the conqueror! He will be strong, he will be a leader, he will have a good life—a good life in America!

Just then James realized how important it was for them to become Americans, not Italians living in America. When he went to America the first time, they had called him James because they had no English word for Biaggio, but his brothers had continued to call him Biaggio, and so had the other Italian people. He had still thought of himself as an Italian.

But now he began to think of himself as James, and soon afterward began demanding that everyone call him James. It was time to make the change, to really become an American, and changing to his American name was a good place to start.

Shortly after, Frank's wife, Josephine, gave birth to their child, Louis. Now both brothers had families waiting for them in Bucita. It was a constant struggle to live each day without living with their wives and knowing their children.

James and Frank had signed up twenty men on their first trip back home to Calabria. Frank had the best results, having spent more time recruiting than James. With the men they brought back to America and those they signed up to come in the following months, they started accumulating a steady stream of cash. Each man they signed up would pay them a sum of money for accepting a mining job. The money they received was actually graft, a common practice among men trying to land a job in America. They also started building homes for the workers and their families, charging mortgages and collecting fees. This was a relief to their Italian countrymen, who would have both a job and a destination awaiting them in America. The Honey Brook Mine Company also paid the brothers for each man they brought and entered on the payroll. Some men signed up in Italy, but never showed up at the mine. Others came to America but stayed in the larger cities, like New York or Philadelphia, where they felt they could find their own futures. Those men became fugitives from the Bruno brothers and it was best for them not to be found.

The brothers knew all too well the sense of longing for home and the old country. So they decided to build in Bunker Hill a large home which to Bucita standards would be a castle. They wanted their wives to be happy and have plenty of room for their families to grow. The house was constructed on the corner of Fourth and Centre Streets on a large lot that the brothers bought after returning as married men. In fact, the lot was large enough for four homes, which would eventually be built. Their brother, Peter, could build a home there also when he came over and if he ever settled on a girl. His teachers back in Bucita always said he was the playful brother; for that matter, so did the girls.

The home of James and Marie Antonia would be set off to one side, at the northeast corner, and Frank and Josephine's would be on the southeast side of the lot. It would be just like in Calabria: the family would be only a doorstep away. Across the street from the two homes was another large lot that the brothers bought for later projects. In the coming years they would purchase plots from the coal companies on the northern and eastern fringes of the village. Land purchases became an important part of their earliest plans. Some homes had already been built on other plots which the coal company still owned and were mortgaged to workers they had brought to the mines. Without this system of mortgages made out to the coal companies or directly to the Bruno brothers, the newcomers would only have had shacks in the dirtiest section of the coal yards.

In the spring of 1883, James returned once again to the land of his birth and now of his son's birth. Frank stayed behind in Pennsylvania because the brothers' business interests were growing quickly and needed supervision. The businesses were too big to be left in the hands of other people.

While in Italy, James signed up many more men to work in the mines of America. He also helped the families of those men already in Pennsylvania to arrange passage for themselves. Many of the men had given money to James to buy passage for their wives and children as well.

Finally, in April, James began the journey back to America for the third time. But this time he was accompanied by Marie Antonia, her first son Francis and their son Joseph, Frank's wife, Josephine, and their son Louis. Now that both their parents were gone, along with Nonno, Peter, the youngest brother in the Bruno family decided it was time for him to go to America, too.

James and Frank both had despaired at not being in Bucita when Nonno passed. They realized that he had never fully recovered from the wagon accident as well as from his wife's passing years earlier. Also their papa had passed within a month after the brothers had left for America. He had become ill with a sickness that resulted from the dampness of a very wet spring.

On the trip home, it was all James could do to be in Bucita on the Via Castil with so many loved ones now gone

Chapter 4

ANOTHER JOURNEY

James was embarking on his third trip to America. He and Frank, still behind in Pennsylvania, had made their plans carefully. They had lived on short rations for months so they could provide the best things possible for their wives and children. No steerage accommodations. Not for their families, not this time.

James was keenly aware of the importance of starting the voyage on the right foot. *A house must have a good foundation to make a good life,* he thought. Not only his life, but the lives of his wife and children, the lives of his brothers and the lives of their families. James believed that a great deal depended on this journey. He felt deeply that the history of the Bruno family would be different from that day forward.

The women of both families had sewn beautiful clothes for the brothers' wives and children, clothes appropriate for their new station in life, according to James. The clothes were more akin to those in the magazines that James had sent to Bucita than anything seen in Calabria. They must not arrive in America looking like the old country they had left behind.

To move forward in their new life, they must begin now, with a fresh start in every way.

The family gathered the new clothing and other possessions and packed them tightly in large containers. Everyone was busy and bustling about, often bumping into one another. Marie picked the baby up and rocked him gently for a few moments. She sang softly to him, "Guiseppe, my baby, my sweet baby boy."

"Stop calling him Guiseppe!" James said sternly to his wife. "It's Joseph, now! Joseph!"

Marie looked up at him and said, "Keep your voice down, James. You will frighten the child calling him by either name. I will call my baby Guiseppe while he is in my arms. My darling baby, my little child of love, *mio bambino d'amore*. It will be time enough to change his name when we are in America."

James flushed at her words and his stern look softened to a smile at the sight of his wife with their baby son in her arms and little Francis hugging her leg. Marie reached for a small package and handed it to James. He looked surprised, then undid the wrappings. The gift was a beautiful leather-bound book to record their journey and the beginning of their life together in the new country.

"I promise to write in it every detail of our journey as often as I can, my Marie," he said softly to his wife.

April 14, 1883 –

Having started our journey today on the road to Napoli, we have stopped for the night. We had a good day traveling, very long though, and everyone is tired, especially the children. We had our meal and now everyone is sleeping, and so must I.

We start early in the morning.

The traveling party was a small one. Included were James, Marie Antonia, with her son Francis, and their young son, Joseph; Josephine, Frank's wife, and their son, Louis, who was the same age as Joseph; and Peter, the younger brother of Frank and James who was emigrating to America for his own chance at a better life. Peter would help with Josephine and Louis on the journey since Frank had remained in America. The brothers' friend Antonio was driving the wagon and would take it home after unloading at the dock in Napoli.

April 16, 1883 –
Today we passed through the village of Sapri in Campania. Everything is so different to me now that I am a man of means. Today I am riding through the very town that I had to walk through so many times before!

April 18, 1883 –
Today we were climbing mountains; not too steep, but the loose stones made it hard to pull the wagon on the narrow dirt road. We arrived in the town of Paeston in time to stop for the night and were glad of it.

I have made this journey twice before. The first time I thought I would never see my country again, and yet here I am leaving it for the third time. My Marie says that we will come back to visit someday when we have made our fortune. It has been so hard, this journey to a new land, a new life. But now I can really believe we will make our fortune. I can do anything with my beautiful Marie by my side!

On the sixth day of the journey to Napoli, a frightening event occurred. Guiseppe, the apple of his family's eyes, was never out of their sight. Barely six months old and not yet walking, he managed to crawl away while the horse rested after the long, hard climb up the mountain. The travelers were eating sausage and bread with a drink of wine. It was quite warm to be so high up and early in the year. Marie lay back down in the wagon on top of some bundles to rest. She nodded off for just a few minutes, not more, then sat bolt upright.

"Where is Joseph? Where is my Guiseppe! My baby!" she cried.

Guiseppe was nowhere to be seen.

Suddenly Antonio saw the baby—he had crawled to the edge of the road and slipped off!

Luckily, the little boy had landed on a small outcropping, but it seemed impossible to reach him. The men would have had to go all the way down the mountain, the mountain they had just climbed.

But Antonio was already on his knees hanging over the edge trying to reach the baby. He almost slipped, too, but James caught the waist of his trousers and together they pulled Joseph back up. Marie was nearly hysterical as Antonio placed her son in her arms. She wept on his little head and soon his smile turned to tears as he caught his mother's hysteria. Everyone crowded around the baby and his mother and soon Josephine and baby Louis were crying as well.

Antonio saved the day yet again by saying everyone sounded like a bad opera and soon they were all laughing at his jokes. His hands were shaking and he was close to tears himself, but he acted strong for the others.

April 21, 1883 –

The trip is taking longer than planned. Climbing up the mountains with the wagon and the women and children is a much different journey than it was for men walking alone. Fortunately for us, there are shepherds watching their flocks in these hills and even if we do not see them, we see the places where they shelter at night, usually near a spring, so we can replenish our water supply. We don't have much to eat but we are used to that, and now we know that it won't be long before we can eat anything we want!

The children are never out of our sight now, with all of us taking turns watching the three young boys.

Sometime the following day, Antonio called to the others,
"Look! You can see Mount Vesuvius in the distance. When we reach Vesuvius, we will be able to see Napoli."

April 22, 1883 –

We have been in sight of the ocean off and on for most of the trip, but today, for the first time, we could see the port of Napoli. Francis was shouting that he could see ships far out on the water, but it was quite hazy and I think it was just his imagination. I should know about that—I've been imagining ships on the ocean my whole life. I remember what it was like to be a child with such dreams.

April 24, 1883 –

Today after almost two weeks we finally arrived in Napoli. It's a good thing we allowed a few extra days for the journey because the day after tomorrow we set sail for America.

Josephine was overwhelmed by the city. She's never been farther than Cosenza. I remember how impressed I was when I saw Napoli for the first time. What will she and Marie think of the great New York City?

Peter and I went to the docks and secured our passage for the voyage. Then we returned to our rooms in the city to wait for the ship to sail. We found Marie, Josephine and the children resting. When everyone was fresh and revived, we found a nice restaurant where we had dinner. It was an extravagance, but it was wonderful. The food in America is good, especially in the Italian restaurants, but there is nothing like a real Italian meal on Italian soil.

"A toast! A toast! Quiet everyone!"

"Yes, Biaggio—James! A toast!"

"Mama!"

"Hush, little baby, Papa is talking!"

Everyone laughed.

"To our wonderful country of Italy, our homeland, our mother country! Long may the sun shine on her shores!"

"May she prosper!"

"May *we* prosper!"

The next morning the family went directly to the ship. Antonio drove the wagon and left the others to board, then went into the city to shop before returning to Bucita. He was the only one to return home from the group that had left on the journey. The family members were sad to see him drive off as he was the last relative they would see for a long while.

"James, come look!" shouted Peter, always the curious one. He was hanging over the railing of the great ship and waving wildly to James. This ship, like the others on which James had sailed, was new and beautiful, white and shining in the sun.

"What is it, Peter?" James called out as he walked slowly up the gangway to the upper deck of the huge ship.

"Our cabins! You won't believe them!" Peter exclaimed with childlike excitement. "We have never had it so fine before!"

The women were already unpacking the trunks, the babies lay sleeping on the beds, and Francis was running from one magical sight to another—the shiny metal walls of the outer decks; the lounge chairs that looked so comfortable and inviting. He loved the hard wooden floors that were so polished he could see his reflection in them and slide along them instead of picking up his feet and walking.

James smiled as he remembered Frank's excitement when they had boarded the ship the first time. That ship had seemed wonderful to those poor country boys then, but the accommodations on this ship left the others far behind.

"You like this, Peter, yes? Do you think you could get used to living like this?"

"Oh, yes, James! I think I could!"

April 25, 1883 –

Even though the ocean liner we are on is not much different from the others I traveled on, it looks completely different from the upper-class decks. I have boasted that I would be successful, I would not be beaten, but now that I am living that success, it can be a little frightening.

Marie is such a help to me, to all of us. She is so comfortable with all this luxury; it is second nature to her. She shows us all what to do, where to go, how to act, what to say. I thank the Blessed Virgin for her every other minute!

April 26, 1883 –

We are finally underway, sailing to America. Well, not sailing exactly, since we are on a steam ship, but going to America we are!

All together and Josephine is beyond excited to be getting closer by the day to her beloved Frank. We said good-bye to Antonio waving to him from the deck as he stood on the docks.

April 27, 1883 –
Last night, at dinner, we were seated at the Captain's table. The captain is Sicilian, and he knew my wife's father. He had seen Marie the night before boarding the ship and they spoke some at the captain's reception. An invitation was delivered to our cabin at dawn and of course we didn't refuse. This is all so different from our first voyage but exactly what I have dreamed of for so long. The dinner was served very late; fashionably late, Marie Antonia tells me.

I was so proud to have my wife, my Marie Antonia, by my side, and grateful, too. There were so many dishes and glasses and pieces of silver that confused me. Only with her help was I able to navigate through the meal. Also, our two sons, Francis and Joseph, were with us for a short time, behaving like gentlemen—if it's possible for ones so young to behave so well.

"Francis, darling, stay away from the railing!"

"But I want to see the water, Mama!"

"Do you want to fall in like Joseph did on the mountain?"

"No, Mama, I won't fall! Look at the birds!"

"They are sea gulls. Look at them searching the water for fish. The fish get hurt by the ship, by the propeller, and then the gulls can catch them."

"James, don't tell him such gruesome stories!"

"It's not gruesome, it's nature. That's how it is in the world and the sooner he knows it the better. Some eat, some get eaten!"

April 28, 1883 –
My Marie speaks beautiful English such as I had never heard from any of my countrymen. She is well-educated because her family sent her to a school where English was spoken.

She has started teaching us English every day after breakfast and dinner. We all gather together—Marie, young Francis running around, little Joseph in my lap or his mama's, Peter, Josephine, and Louis.

I learned many English words in the time I lived in the United States, but I do not speak it well enough to communicate in business. Marie teaches us all the correct way to speak as well as to read and write.

After we practice our English, it's off to bed. Then in the morning at breakfast I help Marie quiz the others about what we learned the night before. At first it was difficult to remember the words but after a few days it became easier for everyone.

"Peter, pay attention! This is important!"

"Oh, James, you know I don't like to study."

"It doesn't matter what you do or don't like. You must learn English! This is our key to freedom and prosperity in America! I am going to need you and depend on you in our businesses. To do that you must learn English and learn it well. Some things never change," James snorted. "You never liked school except when it got you out of field work."

Peter stood up straight, his shoulders back, his chin raised proudly, defiantly, and said, in a combination of Italian and English, "I will learn all I need when I get to America. I will speak English as well as anyone else!"

It was true: Peter was very bright and often learned things after hearing them only once. He was learning the language from other people on the ship—stewards, waiters, and the single women with whom he spent a great deal of time.

April 30, 1883 –

Today, the ship docked in Liverpool, England. We were not allowed to get off, but I stood at the rail looking at the city and the land around it. The city stretched for miles and so many people were there. But the most amazing part was how green the countryside was! Grass and trees—all green! I tell the others it is much like the new place we are going to—Pennsylvania. They tell me that word means the 'woods of Penn,' and that 'Penn' was the man who founded that state. Signor William Penn, our padrone.

"That's the last land we'll see for a long while now. Imagine—10 days without seeing land! What will we do all that time?" Josephine asked.

"You'll study your English, that's what. What's the English word for *mare?*"

James sighed and turned from the rail to Marie, who looked at Josephine expectantly. Peter waved his arm over the rail and shouted, "Ocean!" Josephine looked ashamed that she was beaten by Peter's quick response and started scolding the children in English.

May 1, 1883 –

I am meeting so many people on this trip and many of them are worthy of my time. I am learning many things about this life of style and class, and I am establishing some very important contacts for our future.

Our English classes are so important for our plan. I am able to converse with many of the passengers because my English is better every day.

May 2, 1883 –

Today I met some men who are in politics in the United States. They talked about the election of the president that will come next year. They spoke of the men who want to be president. President! That is better than king, I think!

We talked all afternoon and through dinner and met again on the deck after the women and children had gone to bed.

May 3, 1883 –

I have been writing mostly in Italian, with only a little Inglese, but now there is more Inglese, and soon it will be mostly English!

Mi chiamo Giacomo: My name is James.

Io vado al America: I am going to America.

Marie insegnaro inglese noi: Marie is teaching us English.

"Marie, how do you say, 'My name is James, I am the president?'"

"Why not king, James?" laughed Peter.

"No, not in America. There are no kings in America. President!"

"What a dreamer you are, James!" Josephine said.

"You wait, you will see! If not me, then my son will be president!"

"President of what?"

"America!"

May 4, 1883 –

I was joking a little about being president and perhaps I was just a little serious, too. Why not? I heard someone say that an American farm boy became president of America, so why not an Italian farm boy? But there are many other important positions in America for me and my brothers, my sons and nephews. They can laugh now, but someday I will be someone important in America!

"It has been a pleasure talking with you, Mister Smith. Thank you for helping with the English."

"You speak very well, Mister Bruno. Keep up the good work.

"Thank you, sir. Good day."

"Mister Bruno," James said to Peter. "Did you hear that?"

"Si, Signor Bruno, I hear him!"

"Bah, go back to your old country, Peter, if you don't want to learn the new language!"

"Ah, come now, James, laugh a little bit! You take everything so seriously."

"Yes, yes, I do. It is. But you're right, I do need to laugh, too."

May 5, 1883 –

I spent many hours today with the political men. They have been telling me more about the government of the United States. I have to remember to call it that—its real name, not America.

Some other men joined us today and one was telling how some people who have lived in America, I mean United States, all their lives are against letting more people come in. And these are the ones whose fathers were immigrants! It was all right for their people to go to the new country, but no more. No Italians is what they meant. So this is another battle to be fought, more ugliness to protect my children from. This land of promise, of a bright new day, already has ghosts, bad feelings. So be it. We will still succeed. The Brunos will succeed!

May 6, 1883 –

I lie awake at night thinking about how I can do better, work harder, do more to make a life good enough for Marie and my children. My children must have the education that was denied to me in Italy because of my lowly station in life. My children must never know what it is like to be looked down upon!

"Mummy, look at the little dark children! I want to see them, I want to play with them!"

"Hush, child! Come away from there."

Marie clutched Joseph to her breast and held tightly to Francis's hand as she turned from the rail to go back inside.

"Mama, why wouldn't those children play with us?"

"They had to ... go with their mother."

"What did she say, Marie?"

James was there, his face dark with fury. He had been coming out the door and had witnessed the whole scene, though he had not heard the words.

"Nothing, nothing."

"Tell me."

"Please, James, let's not talk of it."

"It begins. This we will see in America—those who think they are better than us, those who think we don't have the same rights as they do. But we will show them! We are just as good, better!"

"James, lower your voice."

"I have the right ...."

"Yes, you do, but this is not the place. If you want to be respected you have to follow their rules."

James lowered his head stubbornly, but he could not deny Marie's logic. This was hard, harder than he had thought. He knew he would have to fight his way some of the time, but how can you win the fight when you don't know the rules? Or if your enemy won't even look at you, much less talk to you? And there were some of those on the ship, not many, but for every three or four who would converse pleasantly, there was one who would put his nose in the air and turn away.

May 7, 1883 –

I can't believe this! Right here on this ship! We paid our money just like the others did! How dare these people think they are better than me and my wife and children! We will show them! We will! My brothers and me and our children! We will become something in the United States! Them and all their fine ways. They are just men like we are. We have the same chance to succeed as they have and we will! We have that much more determination because we have so far to go and nothing to lose. They do not know how I have already begun to establish our family in Pennsylvania. Even with all the new jobs and many immigrants working side-by-side, I have not seen such prejudice exposed so openly.

James watched the people in the lower decks as they sailed closer to the shores of America. Excitement was growing as they approached their destination. People who had not come out on deck before now haunted the rails, waiting for the first sight of their new homeland. The children were wild with energy, running up and down the deck, shrieking in the wind, frightening their mothers half to death.

"My God, if we get to America with all our children it will be a miracle," Josephine said to Marie, as once again Marie pulled Francis down from the rails.

"Like his Papa?" Josephine asked.

Marie looked at her in question, then understood and nodded. "Yes, like his papa, but also like his step-papa, so excited, expecting so much. I fear for them, both of them," Marie answered.

"Hush, dear. These Bruno men, they have something about them—a power, a determination. My family has lived next to the Brunos on the *Via Castil* back in Bucita for generations. We have always seen them as dreamers."

Marie nodded, watching James talking with some men and gesturing toward the West with one hand, always toward the West, and pulling Francis close to him with his other hand.

James and the others were standing by the railing. James was explaining to his wife and Josephine and Peter that, "those in steerage have to go through a place called Castle Garden."

"We have heard of that, but no one wants to talk about it or what it's like."

"What it's like is a lot of waiting. They ask you many questions like your name and your parents' names and where you're from and what you did there and what you're going to do in America and where you want to go."

"Ha! I want get rich, that's what I want to do!" shouted little Francis.

"Francis!"

James patted him on the back and said, "That's my boy!"

Everyone laughed as James continued, "But the inspectors come on the ship to ask questions to those people with the other classes of passage."

They all nodded as they listened.

"It's very important to do things the right way, right from the start," James said quietly. "The most important thing is to act like you own the place, like you belong, as if you have the right to be there, and to be as successful as the next man, because you do!"

May 9, 1883 –

I am once again close to my new homeland. It still shines somewhere in the distance like a beacon, saying, 'Come home, James, come home.'

We have practiced our English constantly. I have learned more of our new language than in all the time I lived in New York. Marie is a good teacher.

By now we could all pass for longtime residents of New York City. But that will not be enough on which to build a future. We must continue to learn the language and ways of our new surroundings.

"I just know we've left something."

"Don't worry, Marie. We will get new things in America!"

"James! James! Get your feet on the ground!"

"I plan to very soon!"

She laughed, then caught his enthusiasm. He took her hand and turned her around in the little cabin, bumping into the bags and the furniture.

"Oh, you fool! Stop! What will the others think?"

"I don't care! We're almost there! Our new home in America! Our home together!"

May 10, 1883 –

We will dock within the hour. This might be the last time for a while that I will be writing in this journal. Frank will be waiting for us. We will stay in New York for a short time before we take our families to their new home in Pennsylvania.

Marie wants to see more of the city before we go to our new home. She will need to rest. She began to grow tired as the journey progressed until I made her stay in bed with the baby for most of the day. She was so excited, and didn't want to miss anything, but I told her that her health and baby Joseph's health were more important. There will be other journeys.

CHAPTER 5

GETTING SETTLED

James and Frank had planned to move their families to Pennsylvania as soon as they arrived in the United States. But first, the two brothers went ahead to check on their businesses and the new houses. The building had moved slowly because of the hard winter, but the weather was warming up quickly, and with James and Frank back to encourage the builders, construction moved quickly ahead.

Back in New York City, the families were not wasting their time. While James and Frank traveled back and forth from the mountains, Marie continued to teach English to the others. The brothers encouraged Peter to go to school, but he was not interested and exhibited a remarkable persistence for one who had been so carefree and malleable in the past. They told him he had to do something and he agreed. In addition, the brothers felt more confident leaving Peter in the city with their families. So they found him temporary work with Signor Alberti's import company. Peter was an uncle who loved his nephews with all his heart, and he would be sure to protect and help provide for them. Peter could also learn much from Signor Alberti about business American-style. His new-found business knowledge would prove invaluable when he eventually joined his brothers in Pennsylvania.

Eventually the homes were ready. The families had little in the way of possessions, so it was easy for them to get ready to once again leave for a new home. The hard part would be leaving the certainty of an established home among friends in the Italian community of the city. James and Frank told the women that many Irish and Czechoslovakian people lived in the area to which they were going. Also, the number of Italians was growing, many of them having been brought there by the work of James and Frank. Living in a small town in Pennsylvania would be the first time the wives and children would be amongst people foreign to them. But they felt confident that the English Marie had taught them would make them quite capable of conversing with new friends.

So one bright spring day, the entire Bruno family boarded a train and headed for Pennsylvania. The train traveled slowly through the mountains climbing inclines so steep Marie was certain they would slide back down before they reached the top. As the train topped the last mountain separating them from the tiny village where they would make their homes, James and Marie looked down into the valley that held their dreams of a beautiful future.

As they stared at the mountains, James spoke softly, almost to himself.

"There are the hills and the town where we will settle and begin our new lives; the end to a destiny begun with a long journey to New York City from humble Bucita, a journey which led me away from my homeland, my village and my parents, to another land which held a hope, a promise and a pact between brothers to always be there for each other."

Frank added, "A pact that is in our common blood."

James turned from the window to face Marie and took her hands in his.

"Our journey did not stop when we left the ship, but continued as we explored our new country, discovered the riches, the possibilities available here for those willing to work for them. A journey that helped me find myself, find my strengths, my weaknesses, my ambitions. And it was a journey toward you, my dear wife, and to our children, a journey to a better understanding and love for my family. So, after all the time and all the distance, after many long years in the hustle and grime of the city, waiting for the right time to make our move to prosperity and make our family name proud, we now begin our new lives."

Little Joseph, who had screamed until they let him sit by the window where he could watch the scenery, was now on his feet, his little nose pressed to the window glass, scrutinizing the town as it grew closer, and listening to his father's words.

"Home, Papa?"

James smiled proudly at his small but strong-willed son.

"Yes, my son, this is our home, our town. The Brunos' town. Say, that's not bad, Brunostown, Brunotown. What do you think, my dear?" Frank looked at his wife.

"Perhaps we should consider what some of the other residents of the town might think," Marie answered, ever mindful of those around her.

The miners were a strong lot, composed of various ethnic groups including Slavs and Russians, Irish and Czechs. On the whole they were not well educated. Many had made their way from their homelands by working aboard passenger and cargo ships. Some had scraped together enough for third-class passage, then taken low paying jobs to support their growing families. Most of those workers with their varied backgrounds and ways of life had little support from other groups.

The Italians, on the other hand, steeped as they were in the tradition of family and community, helped one another in the early days. Just as the brothers had helped bring fellow Italian men and their families to the small village, they looked out for one another.

The mine workers were appreciative of James's educated and proud-as-a-peacock demeanor; and they recognized that because he had survived the hardships of his past and been given the power to provide for them, the future of everyone in the township was better.

The railroad position that Frank had secured continued to allow him to work closely with Kelly and Ayres. And because the railroad was the lifeline of the collieries, it also provided the brothers with real power. If the rail lines were not extended right to the entrance of a mine, the coal could not be transported economically. So because the placement and upkeep of the rails was part of Frank's authority; it became his decision where and whether or not the lines would be extended.

The Italians in the village were especially grateful for the Bruno brothers as James and Frank offered them the most rewarding opportunities. They admired the Bruno families and were proud of their own heritage and native tongue, which they still spoke in their own homes. Most of the hardworking Italian villagers could barely speak English well enough to function in the town. But in the eyes of the Brunos, the people could see their past. And in the clearly spoken, fluent English the Bruno men spoke with such confidence, they saw a future that was possible for all of them. Frank and James understood those men the best. The Bruno families commanded such respect that it was not uncommon, even on the coldest of days, to see an old man take off his hat in polite greeting.

Next to English, Italian quickly became the most common language spoken on the streets of the village. The village grew rapidly as the brothers built first one and then another street. One street was even named James Street. Out of the surrounding forest emerged new streets on which the Bruno brothers built many houses, then mortgaged them to the immigrant families.

The family itself was growing quickly. The days flew by with all the work there was to do. Marie sometimes felt dizzy and a little sick, especially when she realized the precious time when her babies were small would soon be gone forever. She was torn in her thoughts—wanting the children to grow up and bloom into whatever unique flowers they were destined to be, and at the same time wanted them to stay babies in her arms.

Joseph especially was growing up. He still allowed his mother to kiss him goodnight, but she could see he was beginning to think himself too old for that. His little brother Philip was growing into Joseph's old clothes almost faster than Joseph grew out of them. The little sisters, Lucia and Kandida, were so sweet, imitating their mama and aunties in the way they walked and held their hands. Lucia even wanted a corset, of all things!

"Mama, I want a tiny waist like the girl that works in the dry goods store."

"All too soon, my little lady, you'll be bound into corsets. Don't be rushing yourself!"

Baby Kandida wanted to do everything her big sister did, which both annoyed and delighted Lucia. She loved being admired, but she hated being pestered.

The situation was much the same for Joseph. If he needed lieutenants and soldiers for his games, then everyone was welcome to play. But if another child wanted Joseph to play his game, to follow his lead, Joseph would suddenly lose interest.

James was delighted with his son, "A natural leader! Look at him! They follow him around like he's Garibaldi!"

Marie shook her head, worried that Joseph was becoming arrogant, that she and James were spoiling him. But then he would come to her with something he'd found or a gift he had made for her, and once again, he would be her shining light, almost incapable of doing wrong.

"Do you want a job or not? I have others waiting for the same position that are willing to pay the ten-dollar fee," James told the young man, not unkindly. He looked down at the list of new arrivals to give the man a moment to collect himself.

James realized how confusing everything could seem for them—a long voyage in a dark, crowded ship, the nightmare of the new immigration center at Ellis Island. Ellis Island had replaced Castle Garden which had become too small to handle all the new immigrants. Once off Ellis Island, if they made it past the various exams, awaited the huge bewildering New York City and the wild, sprawling country around it and beyond it. Then a job in a mine, a dangerous job underground, and they wanted him to pay a fee for it, too? Who wouldn't hesitate?

Collecting fees for services rendered was a common practice at that time and most felt it was necessary for them to establish themselves in America. So the newly arrived immigrant and hopeful worker replied, "Of course, I want the job. I need it. I owe you and your brothers so much. You have provided my family safe passage and kept us fed. For this we owe you a great deal of gratitude."

James smiled and extended his hand to the man. He knew most mine officials would never lower themselves to touch a worker, but to James this man was family, he was from Calabria, and though they'd never met, had never even heard of one another, they were kin and James wanted him to feel welcome. He knew the ten dollar fee was steep, but it made the workers feel they had paid for the services they received. If they thought otherwise, they would feel shame that they had been given a handout, like a beggar, and James knew these strong Italian men did not like to feel like beggars. Besides, the men would get the chance to earn that money back and then some. There were plenty of opportunities for an ambitious young man in America. So the man was hired along with four out of ten others in line that day at the office of James Bruno, procurer of labor at the Honey Brook Colliery.

"We've got to get into everyone's pockets, or pants, as the case may be," Frank laughed until James held up his hand so he could continue, "so that everyone is beholden to us. We cater to their needs, and they cater to ours."

Frank nodded in agreement as he watched James place packs of cards and boxes of chips into a leather satchel. James went on, "Of course, we needn't tell them that part."

"No, I know well your passion for secrets," Frank commented.

"We've already done the first and easiest thing to do—started a card game. Next, we work on getting a hall built, for billiards, beer, socializing. I've got a lady in mind, a madam, to set up in a house outside town with a little stable."

"You think of everything, don't you?"

"I can't deny it. I had good teachers," James answered, remembering Signor Alberti and Dominic.

Frank slapped him on the back and said, "I'm sure glad you're my brother! Nonno would be proud of you!"

"Do you really think so?" James asked, stopping suddenly, caught off guard.

"I do indeed!"

James stopped and looked out the window at the mountain slope across the valley and thought of his old grandfather and how important it had been to please him. James fervently hoped that he was living his life in a way that would make Nonno proud.

The room was so full of smoke that someone entering might have thought one of the overstuffed chairs was on fire. But it was just the aromatic smoke of fine Cuban cigars; cigars that James had been given as a going away gift from Luigi. James puffed and thought of that day when Luigi had handed him the cigars.

Luigi had said, "You get your *cosca* started up there in the mountains, Biaggio, and I'll come up and run it for you."

James replied, "Thanks so much, Luigi, you're always so generous. You can be sure I'll call on you."

The two men had laughed and shaken hands for what turned out to be the last time. Luigi was found later that month floating in the East River, wearing the calling card of an enemy *capo*. James thought of Luigi often. Now that his cigars were running out, he thought of opening his own cigar factory in nearby Hazleton.

The three Bruno brothers, Kelly, Ayres, some of Kelly's railroad crew, and a few of the mine supervisors had all gathered in Patrick Kelly's parlor while his wife was in upstate New York visiting relatives. They had been playing cards, but had stopped to call it a night. Kelly and Ayres announced that they were going to join his wife's family in upstate New York and run her family business. Everyone was sad to hear that their two friends would be leaving soon.

"Well, this little town is beginning to look like something, that's sure, but it seems to me it needs a new name," Jack Kelly declared, blowing a cloud of smoke into the air as he pulled back the heavy curtain to expose a view of the darkened street.

"I agree," James said. "Bunker Hill is straight out of the revolution—ancient history, as Joseph would say."

"How about 'Paradise?'" Peter offered, dreamily, lounging in his chair with a glass in one hand and an unlit cigar in the other.

James had opened the cigar factory in Hazelton as planned, employing twenty people, three of them from Cuba, who had the experience and connections to obtain the fine tobacco leaf he imported.

Peter's brothers looked at each other and the other men turned away to hide their smiles. Peter was proving to be not well inclined to work, much to the chagrin of his family. They were constantly racking their brains to find something to interest their young dilettante brother, but so far had been unsuccessful. Patrick Ayres had commented to Kelly that this was one instance when James Bruno was not able to manage things, and ironically, the 'thing' was his own brother.

"I would love to call it 'Bucita' but that would hardly be fair to all the Irish folks who live here," Frank said.

"How about 'Bucita-Clare,' a fine symbol of our melting pot population!" Kelly suggested.

"Aye, an' poetical it be, at that," Ayres rolled the words with a gentle Irish lilt.

"I love the way you do that," James responded, laughing and slapping his friend on the back. "How about 'Ayresville,' or 'Kellyton?'"

"Now 'Ayres' is a mouthful!" Patrick joked and everyone joined him.

"Ah, go back to Ireland, man!"

Kelly noticed that everyone was missing the obvious. "What about 'Brunotown' or Brunoville?" The Brunos are the ones doing so much work around here, providing passage, building houses and adding streets for so many."

"No, no, that wouldn't be any good. Bruno is a fine strong name, but it's not, what did Patrick call it? 'Poetical!'"

"Political, maybe, but not poetical," Frank added, winking at James.

They were all laughing, when Peter said, "Here, I've got it."

The men all looked at him in surprise, as only a minute before he had looked as if he were about to slide under the table.

"Kel-Ayres," he said loudly and got shakily to his feet.

The room was silent as the group of men considered this name, the meaning behind it, the men behind it, and slowly, one by one, began to nod in agreement.

So Peter said it again but with more confidence this time, "Kel-Ayres."

"A fine name!"

"A toast! To Kelly and Ayres, to Kel-Ayres!"

"A toast!" they all responded gaily.

And so the town was named.

"Is that a problem for you, James?" Frank asked as the two men walked home.

"What?"

"The town name, Kelayres. Did you want it to be Brunotown?"

"Yes, I did, when we first arrived. But now I see the value of keeping a low profile, letting others take some of the spotlight."

"You certainly have a lot going on in that head of yours, don't you, James?" Peter caught up with them.

"It's a good thing one of us does, Pete," Frank replied, throwing his arm around his youngest brother to show that he loved him in spite of his laziness.

"I'm just waiting to discover my calling," Peter lamented.

"I've got a suggestion," James countered. "Since you like the alcohol so much, how would you like to be the host in the new hall when we get it built?"

The men looked at one another as they considered the possibility. Frank raised his eyes and then nodded his head. Peter was doubtful, wondering if James had something up his sleeve.

James himself saw the suggestion as a stroke of genius. Peter would get to be sociable, which he did so well, and hopefully they could get him to do a bit of work at the same time. He'd need help at first, but he wasn't stupid—he just had not yet found anything that interested him.

"Would you give it a try, Peter?"

"Well, if you want me to, James. Of course."

"Good. That's settled," James answered and his mind moved on to the issue of whom to invite to another game.

◆　◆　◆

"I'm King of the Mountain!" Joseph stood with his arms raised high on top of a huge slag pile at the high end of the ravine that separated the town from the land owned by the mine. Slag was the leftover rock and debris from the nearby mine.

"You always want to be King of the Mountain! It's not fair!" one of the boys shouted to him.

Joseph's cousin, Louis, stood off to the side, watching, as the other children stood staring up at Joseph.

"Hooray for Joseph, King of the Mountain!" Louis shouted suddenly running into the middle of the group.

"Are you crazy?" a schoolmate asked.

Louis laughed as he thought, Not as crazy as Joe.

Joseph's brother Philip looked back and forth from Joseph to Louis, uncertain about what was going on. Joseph had told him it was his job to do the fighting. But he couldn't see who to fight here. Joseph was looking at Louis, who was looking right back at him, grinning.

Joseph slid down the hill and stopped nose to nose with Louis. "What are you up to?"

"Papa said we need to stick together," he said quietly, so only Joseph and Philip could hear. "We can't all be king, so, since you want to, you be it. I'll be your court advisor and Phil can be your knight."

Louis loved to read and spent as much time as he could with his nose in a book. He had been reading of knights and chivalry and mysterious magicians who were advisors to kings. He realized he rather liked the idea of being in the background, like Merlin, a wise man who knew everything, who stayed out of the middle, out of danger. Let Joe take the brunt of things if he wanted to so much.

"Yeah, okay," Joseph said, though he still was not sure what Louis was up to.

"Trust me," Louis said.

Joseph shrugged and decided it was only right and it was about time Louis saw that. He was the oldest, after all, except for Francis, who didn't count because he wasn't a real Bruno. A rift had begun between Francis and the rest of the brothers. He wanted to be around his mother more and more and the boys were always trying to be with their father. When they all grew older, Francis would move away to school in Philadelphia and marry a girl from there, thus severing his ties with the family.

James came into the dining room where Marie and the children were reading about the Civil War. Kandida, sitting in the corner of the room, looked up from playing with her dolls and shouted, "Papa!"

The other children jumped up from the table and crowded around him.

"Papa, look at my drawing!"

"Papa, you said we could have ice cream tonight!"

"Papa, pick me up!"

"Children, sit down immediately! I have not dismissed you!" Marie called to them

"But Mama, Papa's home!"

James gave Marie a helpless smile as he stood with his arms around his offspring, bouncing and jumping around him.

"Darling, what we really need here is a school. You men can get together to drink and play cards anywhere."

"Oh, we can, can we? And how about your parlor, Signora?"

"James Bruno, sometimes I wonder if your mother had any influence whatsoever on your upbringing!"

"Very little, ma'am. I dropped out of finishing school, ya know!" James raised his hand, pinkie raised as he laughed at his own joke.

Marie frowned and began gathering up her books and papers spread out on the table.

"And I should build a church, too? You said on Sunday a church was a requirement for the moral stability of our fine town," James added, still laughing.

"Yes, and a church! Do you want your children to grow up as wild heathens?"

"I think there's little chance of that, my love, with you in charge," James grabbed Marie. But she broke loose and dropped her burden on the table in the corner. She turned just before going through the kitchen door, and said, "A school, James! Build one!"

"Yes, your majesty!" he replied, bowing low, then leaped across the room to catch her hand again.

"Dear Queen Marie Antoinette! You shall have your school, and your church, and your cake, and eat it, too!"

He refused to let her go, though she struggled in his arms.

"James, I must see about dinner!"

"No, not 'til you kiss me!" James still loved his wife as much as on the day they met.

"James!"

"Marie ...."

"Oh, you devil!"

He laughed then, and kissed her soundly on the mouth.

"James, the children!"

"Indeed!"

As the village had grown, Frank and James had set aside a large plot at the intersection of Centre and Fourth Streets for a proposed church and rectory when the need arose. The lot was situated directly across from James's and Marie's home and diagonally from Frank's and Josephine's.

James needed no reminding that the town needed a church. The church had been an important part of his life, of the community in Bucita. But more than that, the people of Kelayres were clamoring for a church. James could not walk out on the street in the Italian neighborhoods without hearing the women lament that they had to go to McAdoo or Haddock for church. That was not right, they said. Each village should have its own church, just as each village should have its own patron saint.

How does a town go about finding a patron saint? James wondered. A church you can build, but a saint? He'd have to talk to Marie.

So James set about getting the church built. He knew about finding workers. He was still finding workers for the mine, so now he also looked for builders, carvers, stone masons—Italian, of course, or Irish if no Italians were to be found.

But James met his match with the Church. He quickly realized that building a church was not a project he could run with an iron fist as he did his own businesses. The priests were happy to take his money, the stone he procured, the stone masons he found, and occasionally even listened to what he wanted. But in the meantime, they did it their own way and in their own time, and the wheels of an organization as old as the Catholic Church moved very slowly.

"He did it again!" James complained to Marie. "He smiled and took my money and shook my hand and listened and agreed and said, 'Of course, of course, Signor Bruno, we all want the best for the church.' Then he went right back doing it the way I told him not to!"

"Darling, it's the Church. Do you really think you should try to change it?"

"I'm paying enough to have a say in it, damn it!"

"Oh, James, don't swear! Especially not about the church. You should give your money gladly, with open hands and an open heart."

"Yes, Marie, you're right, I should."

She smiled broadly at him and took his hand, but her smile faded at the look on his face.

"But I can't!" he shouted and stormed out of the room.

Shortly after, Frank took over the supervision of the church building. But James helped him name the church—the Immaculate Conception Italian Church.

"James! Would you want your son, our Joseph, working in the mines?"

"No, of course not, but this is different. These people need the money their children earn. We don't."

"Children shouldn't have to work. They should be in school."

"Yes, my dear, I agree, but the families have to eat!"

"Well, they could eat if the mining companies didn't take all their money! It's slavery!"

As much as James loved his beautiful and volatile wife, he sometimes wished she were more docile, more like Josephine, a wife who knew her place. What had her parents been thinking when they'd named her Marie Antonia? Now she thinks she's a queen! It was one thing to joke about it, but quite another when she acted the part.

"It will all change soon enough. What with the laws and the unions, nothing is going to be allowed to stay the same."

"That's as it should be."

"Just as long as they don't do something ridiculous like giving women the vote."

"James!"

"Marie, I was joking, I was teasing you!"

"That's not funny!"

"I see, I see. I'm sorry!"

Because of his frustration over the church, James was making life difficult for everyone. Frank and Marie talked it over and decided that to distract him, Marie would suggest that James begin planning the school. It was exactly what he needed.

Some of the townspeople were arguing that they didn't need a big school, just two or three rooms. That was really all they could afford and would be plenty big enough because so many children didn't go to school as they worked in the mines. And those that went to school did so in nearby towns, like McAdoo.

Marie and Frank looked at each other, wondering if they had gotten James out of the frying pan and into the fire. But James did not even notice the little problem.

"No, it would be foolish to build a small school when we'll just outgrow it in a year or two. The children won't be working in the mines much longer. The laws will soon be enforced. I have plans for an excellent school here. We'll come up with the money somehow." James' confidence won the people over and plans proceeded under his direction.

Of course it had to be the best school in the county. Brick to stand the tests of time, fifteen rooms, a coal furnace, all the modern conveniences, windows looking out at the mountains. James did not want his children closed in dark classrooms. And of course, the Brunos controlled all the building contracts and made sure it was built the right way, their way. Unlike the church, James thought.

The school was soon finished and dedicated and was a fine example of a comfortable, heated facility. Many claimed it was too large and costly, but the school district closed two outdated schools, one in Lofty and the other in Black Hills, to fill its rooms. Then James acquired school buses to transport the school children from those remote hamlets.

The church was eventually finished, too. That was not the end of it, though, because even the dedication of the church proved difficult. The women wanted a parade and an old-country festival. They had been growing flowers just for the occasion, and it looked as if it was going to be perfectly timed, with all the flowers blooming or at least in bud at just the right moment. Unfortunately, two days before the big event, someone had furtively gone through the gardens and cut off most of the flower heads.

But the vandal or vandals had not ruined all the gardens. Some had dogs tied up in them; others were out of reach. The women were able to create most of the decorations with what was left, and congregations from other towns donated some of their flowers to make up the difference.

Everyone talked about who would do such a thing, but no one knew for sure. Plenty of people around had started to resent the Brunos. They were the envy of many, and envy can make people act rashly. James had a strong idea of who had demolished their gardens and was ready to punish them, but Marie was adamant and prevailed.

"This has already gone too far for an event that is supposed to be a celebration of love and faith. It's about the church, not us," she told him firmly.

"But Marie ...."

"James, you will do nothing. Do you hear me?"

"Marie, you can't give me orders. It doesn't look right. This is a matter of saving face."

"James, if you lead in this, the other men will follow you. Set an example, not just for your men or the town, but for your sons."

James sighed, knowing that when Marie invoked their sons he was defeated.

Meanwhile, the *Hazelton Daily Standard, July 17, 1899*, said it all:

> Though seriously handicapped at
> times these good people strove
> and labored amidst the most
> disheartening obstacles and the
> most trying circumstances, never
> for a moment becoming discouraged
> or chilled in their unwavering
> Christian ardor to achieve that
> object which had its consummation
> yesterday in the dedication of
> the new holy structure.

The dedication of the Immaculate Conception Italian Church was a huge success. Since he had directed the final stages of construction, Frank was chosen as Grand Marshall for the big event. With James by his side he led the parade on horseback through the streets of the village. All the people were delighted to have their own church. And the picnic lunch on the church grounds was enjoyed by all.

Though James had told Joseph the story of Garibaldi and the red shirt army, Joseph was more interested in American leaders. George Washington was all right. Ben Franklin was better— all those things he had invented and the exciting life he lived. Thomas Jefferson had his elegant home, Alexander Hamilton had been a dashing soldier, but then he'd gone and gotten himself killed, although in a duel, which was exciting.

Joseph pondered the slogans of the revolutions. *Roma o morte* and "Give me liberty or give me death!" He found it hard to imagine having to make such a choice. Who would dare to threaten his liberty or his life?

When Joseph studied about such things, it seemed like ancient history. But the men he read about in the newspapers, who were reshaping the country into what they called an industrial giant, the men who owned the railroads and mines that his father and his uncles worked for, wielding so much power and money that not even the United States government could control them—those men were Joseph's idea of heroes. James laughed to hear Joseph recite the events of the day practically verbatim from the newspaper, his young face glowing as he talked of the latest conquests of Carnegie and Morgan and Rockefeller.

James was thrilled to see his son so interested, so articulate on the matters of money and politics, yet able to talk Italian at home and participate with his uncles when they talked business.

"He will be the leader I've trained him to be," James said to Marie. "To get the best education possible, Joseph needs to go to the boarding school in Hershey."

"No."

"But you want him to have an education?"

"Yes, of course, I do, but he can get a fine education right here. Anything he doesn't learn at school, we can teach him."

"But Hershey is one of the best schools in the country. He could go anywhere and do anything he wanted with an education from there."

"No."

James studied Marie's face as she looked down at the work in her lap. He could tell this was important to her because she was holding her work, not actually sewing. Her hands were only idle when her mind was working too fast for her to do both.

"Why not?"

"James, I know what it's like to be sent away to school. It's terrible. And I went to a school where I was accepted, where I was the same religion and nationality and class as the other girls there. What would it be like for him to be the only Italian boy, the only Catholic boy, the only working-class boy in the whole school? Think of that. Do you want to subject him to that?"

"What I want is for him to have the best education possible. I want him to be able to do anything he wants to when he grows up."

"You want him to be president."

James looked away. He could hear the accusation in her voice, telling him he was being unrealistic, again, that he was putting all his own ambitions on this one young son. Well, damn it, yes, he was! He did want Joseph to be president! And why not? Why the hell not?

"Why the hell shouldn't I?"

"You said you want him to be able to do what he wants to do, that's why—not what you want him to do."

"I want him to have that option."

"James, I want him to have everything, too, the best, every opportunity. But I also want him to be happy, not just driven."

He knew that when she took a stand like this, she felt very strongly. Usually she deferred to him and let things flow along. He decided the best thing was to let it ride for now, maybe even feel Joseph out, see how he felt. Yes, that was it. If Joseph wanted something, he could get his mother to agree.

"All right, my dear, if you say so," he said biding his time.

Marie looked up at James, but she did not smile. She knew that tone of voice only meant an armed truce, a lull in the fighting. She would soon find out what he had in mind.

Peter was doing well with his assignments. James soon realized that it had been a stroke of genius to put Peter behind the bar. He was well-liked and, as it turned out, he had a head for that kind of business. He knew what to order and when; he knew how to handle people. He could get them laughing, keep them from fighting. The responsibility of the position had caused Peter to grow up almost overnight. He had also played an active role in starting the volunteer fire department and served as a fireman, a position that James suspected he liked even better than running the hall.

When things were quiet in the hall, Peter would practice his billiard game, and he had become quite an expert. A couple of men from Philly had come up to try their luck with the local champ, much to Peter's delight and James's astonishment.

"Well, after all, he is a Bruno," Frank said, as he watched Peter wipe the table clean, leaving the sharps from the city with their mouths open, and their pockets empty.

"No, Papa, I don't want to go away to that school. I want to stay here and learn from you and Uncle Frank and Uncle Peter. I'm ready to go to work. I've had enough of school."

"You have not had enough schooling yet, Joseph."

"Joe, Papa, I'm Joe now. I'm almost a man."

"You're twelve years old, for God's sake!"

"Thirteen, Papa. Don't swear in the house. You know Mama doesn't like it."

James spluttered, but Joseph continued.

"You were working when you were much younger than me, Papa."

"That was different! I want you to have the best education possible!"

"I have a fine education, Papa. Now it's time for me to learn the business."

James shook his head and wondered what he had spawned.

Around the turn of the century, as Joseph continued to grow and the family business blossomed, the tiny thrown-together shanties of the mining village of what had once been Bunker Hill, had become a true community. Kelayres had mushroomed as the Bruno brothers built more houses for their fellow immigrants on the eastern and northern boundaries. They filled the new homes with Italians, but not as many came from Calabria as earlier. As times were getting tough in Italy and news spread of the opportunities in America, Italians were also coming from Sicily and the northern parts of Italy.

A small grocery store called Lotsi Pears and a drugstore named Saladago's opened for business just around the corner from the Bruno homes. The brothers provided many services to the townspeople. The government started to provide some services as well. A post office was opened in the first floor of a cousin's home on the opposite corner from the church, and in 1899 Frank's brother was named postmaster.

Of course the brothers' services were not free—everything cost money, and someone had to pay. Many of the settlers had no money when they arrived, but the brothers would rent the homes they had built on Third Street and later on Fifth Street. These homes were also available to purchase, which many of the immigrants were able to do after just a few years in town.

The next logical step was to open a mortgage company, so the brothers opened The Miners Mortgage Company in neighboring McAdoo. The company was on Main Street near the intersection where the Kelayres road came into McAdoo. The workers living in McAdoo, Kelayres and other nearby villages could pass the offices on the way home from the mines with paychecks in hand. The brothers continued to loan money to the families through the bank at standard mortgage rates. Many families were so short of money that the brothers at times bought shoes or coats for the children so they could attend school. Getting the children to school was of utmost importance to James. It was clear to him that without an education, the future of these children in America would be the same as it would have been in Italy, as it had been for him and his brothers.

Some families would get into money troubles and the brothers would help them out by loaning money at a fee. In this way many villagers felt obligated to them, and others felt a strong bond.

While the mines were running, the town grew and the number of people owing the family multiplied. When the mines were not running, those that were not connected usually fell behind and moved away to other areas, searching for work in a faraway mine. They had no one to turn to for support or to hold them over until the mine was running at full capacity again.

"James, we're just going to have to learn to live with it," Frank said, looking up from his newspaper article on the mining strikes.

"No, we're not. The big men aren't. Why the hell should we?"

"Well, let the big men take care of the problem then. What can we do?"

What indeed, James wondered. The union seemed to have a stranglehold on things, and no one was getting anything done. It wasn't as much of a problem for the Brunos because their other businesses continued even when the mines weren't running. But lots of people went further into debt when the workers could not cross the picket lines and James did not like it. He wanted everything to run smoothly, for the workers to go to work, for the women to shop and cook, for the children to go to school. And for those who needed it to have a little sip or a little game of chance, a little pleasure. And all those things cost money.

If James thought the strikes were bad, the depression that followed was worse. How had the government and the men running these huge companies let things get in this condition? He might as well be back in Italy.

And the newspapers—telling the tale, two tales, really, of life in America. There were the rich, the wealthy, as they called themselves, living with the best of everything—food, wine, cars, art, entertainment, homes. And then there were the poor, who had almost nothing. They talked of the class in between, the middle class, who were just that, in the middle, and had enough to eat, to wear, to live in, and sometimes a few luxuries as well.

But in a small mining town, there were not that many of the upper two classes. The wealthy, the owners, didn't live anywhere near the mines. They were down in Philadelphia, upstate New York, or even in New York City somewhere along the Hudson. As for the middle class, James had difficulty picturing any of them in Kelayres. Well, perhaps he could include store owners, the blacksmith, teachers, lawyers, professional men; the men whose children attended school.

James knew he had lived through worse, and with a whole lot less than he had now. He had plenty of irons in the fire, so fortunately he was not dependent on any one thing. And he was just about to add another iron to it all.

CHAPTER 6

POLITICS

The banner on the building read, "Elect James Bruno as Tax Assessor on Tuesday." Around the corner was another banner: "Peter Bruno for Squire." And farther down the street, yet another, "Vote Frank Bruno—Kline Township School Director."

The three Bruno brothers had decided it was time to take advantage of their positions at the mine. Ninety percent of the male population worked in or had some connection to the mines, the railroad and the hall where they also socialized. The brothers were hopeful that such positions would provide them with a good opportunity to spread their political influence.

Once again, they were correct. The air of authority each carried in his respective place of business as well as the positions of stature all three held in the community had worked in their favor. The three brothers all swept to victory. Frank was named chairman of the Kline Township Republican party which provided him an opportunity to spread the family influence even further.

The number of loans the brothers held in the community did not hurt either. The Miners Mortgage Company was now one of the largest in the area having just completed a brand new building.

James had always loved a challenge and he always demanded respect. Both were afforded him in his new position. The position also provided a way for James and his brothers to insert themselves into that inner circle of power, politics, and government, and to truly begin this mountain *cosca* that could then rule with little fear of reprisals.

"You can get a lot accomplished when no one is looking in your direction," James said to Frank and Peter, as they sat smoking and sipping their dark red wine the night after the election. They had just finished a long day and evening of celebration with friends and families and had barely managed to walk away from tables heavily laden with rich and delicious foods from the varied heritages of the townspeople.

"We're having a hell of a time and we're the shining light of this little community, but we still need more territory if we are going to be a contender in the region," James told his brothers.

"Aye, a shining light, James, I'll drink to that," Peter said, lifting his glass to his brother. "On the other hand, if you're a shining light there's a danger that they'll all start looking in your direction."

Frank laughed and said, "He's got you there, James!"

Peter was now a full-fledged, hard-working member of the family. He had already opened several pool halls and added slot machines throughout the county. In fact, the old mortgage building in McAdoo was now a saloon and pool hall James took Peter's teasing in stride. He had earned the right to say what he thought. *Besides, he keeps me honest,* James reasoned.

James continued, "We'll just have to keep one step ahead of them. There are other elements to get our hands on now. We need slots, the numbers racket, and more card games all over the valley."

Frank nodded, his head heavy not only from all the excitement and celebrating, but also the weeks of campaigning and preparing for the election. Only James would be thinking up more things to do, tonight of all nights. Their sister Lucia had recently been named as postmistress of Kelayres by the president replacing Frank. That had given James some ideas, but as of yet nothing had come of them.

"And real estate, there's always money in land. Land is as solid as gold."

"Banking," Peter added. "Gold is solid as gold." The three brothers laughed and toasted each other.

At the same time, James's son Joseph was struggling to live up to the ideals of his parents. His mother doted on him, and his father pushed him to be better and better. Joseph wanted nothing more than to work in the business with his father and uncles, but James was reluctant to even discuss most of the facets of the Bruno family empire with his young son. Joseph didn't care. He was still the headstrong, determined person he had been as a young child. He was already creating an empire of his own, hoping to someday, in the near future, rise in his father's esteem enough to be initiated into the *cosca*.

Joseph knew his father had struggled and worked hard his whole life. He had climbed up from nothing and continued to strive, to never rest. The family had not been poor when Joseph was born, but certainly not rich either. Joseph knew his father continued to work, to expand his businesses and connections, wanting to give his family the best of everything. So as Joseph grew up, his family's lifestyle improved steadily. By the time he was in high school, his family was much better off than most families in the region.

"You think you're something special, don't you? Just 'cause your father and his brothers think they run this town that makes you a hotshot?" some children taunted.

"They do run this town and I am special. And don't you forget it," Joseph answered.

"Yeah, right. Joe Bruno is something special. Big Joe Bruno. Five feet two inches tall Big Joe Bruno."

"Take it back."

"I won't."

"Phil ..."

"Can't even fight your own fights, can you? Shorty! Big Joe, Big Joe!"

"Don't talk to my brother like that. I don't like it,"

Philip stood up, though not much taller than his brother, he was a big boy and could be intimidating when he looked an opponent right in the eye and held his broad hands in fists in front of him.

"Sure, two against one. No fair."

"That's how it is with the Brunos. We're family. We stick together. We run this town; we run this school. You better remember that."

Philip was learning to take advantage of his size to make his way in the world, and he was constantly working to increase his strength—lifting weights, carrying heavy things—and fighting whenever he got the chance, which was often enough.

"I've got a ten on McAdoo," Joseph said quietly to Louis who nodded.

They were talking in the dim hall during the school lunch break, strategically standing near a classmate they were attempting to hook. He was the son of a man who owned a big clothing store, the kid with the most spending money in the whole school, and none too bright, in Joseph's opinion.

"You're betting against your own school?" the boy asked incredulously.

"Of course. McAdoo is gonna beat the pants off us. Why shouldn't I make some money on it? Somebody should get some good out of it."

"Oh. Does ... I mean, that is ... does this sort of thing go on a lot?"

Joseph shrugged, Louis smiled and Phil quietly moved in behind the boy.

"Can anyone get in on it?"

"Why? Do you want a piece of the action?"

"Well, maybe."

"Sure I like you. I like you just fine," Joseph was busy collecting his books after class, feigning disinterest in the pretty girl standing at his side.

"Then why won't you go to the dance with me?" She tried unsuccessfully to keep the pleading out of her voice.

"I just don't want to, that's all."

"Joe Bruno, you're just mean, that's all! Stuck up!"

"I am not stuck up. I got other things to do than go to dances. I sat with you at the picnic, didn't I? What more do you want?"

"I want you to go to the dance with me!"

"Girls!" Joseph walked off, joining Louis, who was waiting for him. When he was sure Joseph's back was turned, Louis winked and smiled at the girl standing in the hall.

"He makes me so mad sometimes! I wish I could just forget about him!" The girl had run down the hall to where her girlfriend was waiting.

"Well, why can't you?" The other girl shook her head as she buttoned her coat.

"Because he can be so nice. When he's not being so mean, that is."

"You're just a fool," her friend laughed.

"Oh, I don't know about that. The girl that lands Joe Bruno would be sitting pretty."

"The girl that lands Joe Bruno will have to practically be the Queen of Italy and would already be sitting pretty even to get his attention."

"He's like you, James. The work is more important to him now, at least until he meets the girl who'll knock him off his feet, like Marie did to you," Peter said, smiling as he watched Joseph talking to the men and ignoring the girls looking for dance partners.

"I never got knocked off my feet by anything!"

"That's right, James," Frank shot back. "You didn't spend that whole first year we were in America mooning about her, your nose to the grindstone, trying to forget her."

"And sailed right back home the minute you heard she was free again," added Peter.

"Humph," James mumbled, looking at Joseph. "I went back for business, Peter, you know that."

"Yes, James, of course you did."

Sometimes the deck is not dealt as fairly as one believes. As fate would have it, James and his family were being dealt a great hand at the turn of the century. The new century was shining like the pages of an unwritten book for the Bruno brothers and their families, waiting for them to write in it their story of success.

The men in the family were diving into politics in three important arenas—control of money and political power with James as tax assessor; control of governing and political power with Peter as town squire; and control of schools with Frank on the school board.

On the other hand, they were gaining more and more varied and widespread involvement in their other businesses, both legal and illegal, as well as those on the murky boundary between the two. Frank had just opened a clothing store in McAdoo. Gambling and prostitution were going strong and spreading throughout the valley. The brothers were buying or controlling more and more of the houses they rented or sold to the miners. They had become the primary bankers of the town, always willing to lend a hand to the needy, yet trusting, immigrants.

James strolled down the street, whistling, his hat set at a jaunty angle, his new suit pressed and sharp. He was feeling better than he ever had in his life. Everything was going so well. A lot of what the brothers did might look like luck to an outsider, but James knew the hard work they all had put into their success. Sometimes a little luck came their way, too, though, and James was not such a fool as to look a gift horse in the mouth. He was on his way to take advantage of just such a gift. It turned out that the luncheonette next to the park was available, and he saw it could easily be adapted to his purposes, as so often seemed to happen.

The deal set, James returned to his home, deciding as he walked that it was time to let his son Joseph in on the brothers' plans and to decide what his place was to be in them.

The time had come to expand their gambling operation outside the valley. Though the Bruno brothers had set up games for the locals, there was not much going on in the other towns in the region—most of the high rolling was taking place down in Philadelphia or New York. Now was the time to expand and build a reputation of good, high level gambling right here in the coal region where the potential for being uncovered was slim.

Only a few members of the inner Bruno circle knew of the net that was about to be cast on the unwitting community, that coal diggers and colliers were about to lose their shirts. Of course not all of them would—someone has to win, sometimes, and some would gain from all this, further helping to establish James and his family.

The number of slots and game tables swelled over the following months until it seemed the whole valley was gambling. The difference was that outsiders were coming to Kelayres to play instead of the local people taking their wages to the city. The slots were kept mobile in case of a raid and for ready availability at the many different sites. For a man to have a winning night in McAdoo one night, and a lose-your-shirt night in Pottsville the next was not unusual.

As director of schools, Frank Bruno was responsible for the school bus. He made the decision to park the bus in the garage of James Bruno, with the school, of course, paying for its use. The bus was then readily available whenever the need arose. Not ones to waste resources, the Bruno brothers put the idle bus to use for hauling the slot machines during off hours to where the demand was the highest.

Joseph was walking tall, his shoulders back, his chest out, looking every inch a proud Bruno. He was on a mission, a Bruno family mission. Finally, his father and his uncles were letting him in on the action, letting him into the business, and, he hoped, soon letting him out of the filthy coal mine work. Even though he did not actually work in the mine, just going there with his father, with the foremen and managers, he got dirty anyway. He breathed the coal dust in spite of himself and he hated it.

Today was different. Joe was doing real business, real family business. He would complete his assignment, then stop at the soda shop on the way back to see if any of his friends were there, Even though he couldn't tell them what he had been doing, he felt certain that an aura of importance would surround him, that he would look taller, older, and somehow more important.

Just outside the building where he was supposed to meet the family friend, he caught sight of a girl he had never seen. She was a tiny, delicate little thing, with a perfect face, just like a doll. Why had he not seen her before? Where on earth had she come from? The area was growing fast, it was true, but still, how could he have missed such a beautiful girl? Joe stood staring at her, unaware of people and traffic passing around him. She was with an older woman, probably her mother, but Joseph had eyes only for the girl.

"Joe, there you are! Come in, come in!" The man he was meeting took him by the arm and pulled him toward the shop door. Joseph turned once more to look at the strange girl and vowed, I'm going to marry that girl.

"All the signs point to him," James said quietly.

"It sure does look like it. It doesn't make sense though," Frank said, frowning and shaking his head.

"What? Of course it does. He's been out to get us since he opened that place."

A fair-sized amount of Bruno liquor had disappeared and what little evidence there was appeared to lead to a competitor who had a small tavern on the edge of the next town.

"But to do something so obvious. I don't know, it just doesn't make sense to me."

"We'll just ask him, how's that?"

James had had a run-in with the man a few years back and had never forgotten it. He saw this as payback and James wanted revenge.

"Ask him? What are you planning, James?"

"Just, you know, take him aside, ask him what he's planning to do with it. How the hell does he think he can sell liquor that's obviously ours in our town?"

"Ask him, is it? With a baseball bat?"

"Maybe. We might need some sort of persuasion tool. We'll just have to see what the situation calls for."

"I just hope it don't rain so hard that the roof caves in."

"Don't be wishing for bad luck, now. It'll all be fine, you'll see."

James and Frank and some others were setting up the slots under a tent in a small grove of oaks behind the church. At the same time the women were laying out dishes of salads with mozzarella and tomatoes, a variety of pastas with different sauces, meatballs, sausages, spinach with garlic, and on and on. Soon the tables were in front of the church beneath tents the men had set up earlier overloaded with the specialty dishes. So much food was there that additional tables had to be set up along the side of the tent for the fabulous desserts: cannoli, *pizzellas,* rum cake, and more.

"The Lord giveth, and the Lord taketh away," James said, laughing at his own joke. The men would stuff themselves with the homemade specialties, then come back to the woods to divest themselves of their pocket money.

"James, don't go tempting the fates now. It's bad enough we do this, there's no need to flaunt it."

"Aye, Frankie, you're right. I'll be still now," James laughed as he hoisted another of the heavy machines from the back of the van. "I'm a blessed man and I am sorely grateful for it. Thank you, Lord!"

"You like your fine clothes well enough, don't you, your furs and your cars, and your nice house? You want your children to have the best of everything, everything you didn't have? Where do you think that kind of money comes from? It doesn't grow on trees, little lady, I can promise you that. Neither does your fine Catholic God leave it in a basket on the front step."

Peter's wife stood in front of James, hands in fists on her hips, her face red with fury.

"James Bruno, that's blasphemy! I know you encourage these poor souls to gamble away their pay, and drink it up, but at the church! At the festivals of the blessed saints! How could you?"

"God gets his share. We always tithe our ten percent to the Good Father. And we stay out of sight. At least this way the men attend the festivals. If we didn't set up there, they'd just go to the halls leaving the little woman and kiddies to make their own way."

"You have no shame!"

"I'd say that makes two of us, ma'am."

"But who is this girl, Joseph? Where does she come from, who is her family?"

James and Marie stood behind their son's chair where he sat eating a late supper. He kept his own hours these days, and Marie seldom knew anymore where he was or when he might come in.

"We are her family."

James and Marie looked at each other over his head, then stepped back as he suddenly rose from his chair.

"That was delicious, Mama, as always. I just hope Cecilia can cook as well as you—but then, she'll have you to teach her."

Joe kissed his mother's cheek, pushed in his chair, and turned to his father.

"I have those figures that we were discussing, Papa. Would you like to talk about them later tonight?"

"Ah, yes, son, yes. That would be fine."

"I'll be back around ten. We can talk then," Joseph patted his father's back and was gone.

James and Marie looked at each other again.

"Well, we raised him to be proud of himself," James said, frowning.

"Yes, we did. And to be a leader," Marie replied, taking James's hand.

"Yes, we did," he said. "We certainly did."

Joseph had invited Cecilia and her mother to sit with his family at church, and afterward, to join them for dinner. Mrs. Cosimo Rizzuto had declined but only because they had a previous invitation. Of course this meant another day without Cecilia.

"Joseph, there are some things that one does not do until one is married," Marie spoke in her strong tone as they walked home. She was not going to let this young man who was her son, and who had become so grown-up all of a sudden, intimidate her.

"Well, I'm going to marry her, sooner or later, so let's just make it sooner."

"It's probably better that way. Keep you out of trouble," James said.

"James!"

"Well, Marie, you said yourself children are so wild these days."

"Don't talk that way in front of him!"

"He knows what we're talking about, don't you, Joe?"

Joseph bent to kiss his mother's cheek, then opened the front door for her.

"I'll be back later with Cecilia ... and her mother. We'll talk about a date then."

"James, he's so young! And Cecilia's still a child!" Marie went to the window to watch Joseph walk down the street.

"Some child," James said softly, thinking of the beautiful young woman Joseph had brought home for them to meet just a few short months ago.

"James Bruno!"

Not too long afterward, Cecilia's father, Alphonso Rizzuto, gave permission and signed the necessary papers for his young daughter to marry Joseph. Cecilia was only 16 and Joseph was 18. Apparently it was love at first sight, not to be denied. Joseph's Uncle Peter, as town squire, signed for the state of Pennsylvania. The wedding was on, just as Joseph had predicted the first time his eyes came upon Cecilia. Cosimo and Marie wasted no time in arranging the ceremony and planning every detail of the grand reception.

The Bruno-Rizzuto wedding day was a day the village would long remember. The couple emerged from the church to a crowd of more or less the entire local population. Everyone was throwing coins and flowers as the newlyweds rushed forward and climbed into the waiting horse-drawn carriage—a picture right out of a fairytale. The couple was paraded around town and into McAdoo, where the reception was held at the Knights of Columbus Hall. The much-coveted invitations were not to be dismissed, and everyone had plenty to tell afterward. No expense had been spared: the food alone could have fed two villages. In fact, dishes of pasta and cake were sent outside to feed the gathered crowds.

"I told you it didn't make sense for him to have stolen that liquor from us, I told you!" Frank accused James loudly.

"Yes, I guess you were right."

"You guess?' Frank was almost breathless. "The man's in the hospital and we found the liquor on the other side of town from his place and you guess I was right?"

"We all make mistakes."

"James ...."

"Forget about it, Frank." James shrugged, and turned away.

Frank shook his head. He did not always agree with James but he had always had a difficult time standing up to him.

"Well, what the hell are we gonna do with him? The town will have our hides if we hurt the little gimp," James pounded his fist in his hand, looking through the window at the young crippled man tied to a chair inside. He had somehow gotten his hands on some slot machines and set them up in an abandoned shack located on the road to town leading from the mine. The miners had to pass his place first, before getting to the Bruno establishment, and too many of them had been stopping. The Bruno men could not allow such competition in their own territory. And it would not do to show such a loss of face.

"Damned if I know." Frank was more shaken than he liked to admit. Knocking around a man who could defend himself was one thing; a man who could earn his own way and who should know better. But what can be done to a cripple?

"I say let's put 'im to work for us. If he wants so bad to work with the slots, let's get him with us instead of against us," Peter spoke for the first time.

James looked at his younger brother with a new respect. He seemed to be living up to his position as the town squire, learning a lot about power and control, but also about working with people. And he brought all that home to his brothers, to the family business.

"Well, sure, if he'd go for it."

"He'll go for it. Hell, he thinks we're going to kill him now."

"Why didn't he think about that two weeks ago when he got his hands on our slots, the damn fool?"

"Maybe he had this all planned."

"Maybe pigs can fly, too, Pete. But not bloody likely."

The more influence and power the Bruno brothers gained, the more businesses and positions they held simply increased the frequency of problems and their troubles multiplied. There was always an incident to look into and a problem to be solved. That was why having the whole family together always proved so important.

"Have you heard what they're saying?" James was angry. "It was all just an amusing joke played on the Brunos by several fun-loving boys. We're criminals because we supply these people with the opportunity to gamble, which they would do whether we had anything to do with it or not, but these 'boys,' these 'fun-loving boys,' are 'innocent!' God help me!"

"Cool down, James, think of your heart."

"I am thinking of my heart! Those thieving swine stole from us! From the Brunos! We don't have to take this lying down!"

"It was just a bunch of kids. It's just the sort of trick Joe and Louis would pull, and then you would think it was funny."

"It was stealing, plain and simple. But because it was from slot machines, our slot machines, we're the bad guys!"

"Those kids shouldn't have been anywhere near that hall in the first place. They should have been in school, shouldn't they?" Peter asked.

"No, they're older than that," Frank replied.

"Innocent, my foot!" James stamped his foot to emphasize his point.

"Where do you get slugs like that, anyway?" Peter asked.

"I think one of them works in a machine shop and he probably made 'em there."

"The other two are just off the ship. They don't even speak English yet."

"All right, all right. So what are we going to do with these 'innocent, fun-loving boys?'"

The young peasant immigrant did not realize what he had done until his nose and arm had been rearranged for him, helping him to see more clearly how things worked in this valley. He pleaded his innocence, stammering bits of English interspersed with the seeming gibberish of his mother tongue, begging for mercy, but his stupidity was of no concern to the powerful man. The man, representing his employers, would make sure that the boy got his lesson, a lesson that others could easily see with a glance in the boy's direction as he limped down a street or tried to carry his coal to the cart.

"It is my right. You are my property, my wife. You shall do as I say."

Cecilia was stunned into silence at this change in her husband and shocked at his words. James and she had often had small disagreements in their young marriage. Perhaps Cecilia had been too young a bride at sixteen. They argued about many things but mostly about the businesses that dealt with prostitution and gambling. Joseph, it seemed, did not share his wife's point-of-view and soon after Joseph's frequent outbursts, Cecilia quickly learned to keep her opinions to herself.

In the bright sunlight of the next morning, he was once again the mild, charming Joseph that Cecilia knew. But she noted a difference now, a shift in his attitude. He had shown her that he was on top, even with her, and there was no discussion or debate on these issues. She remembered what his cousin Louis called him— King of the Mountain.

Joseph had not laughed or even smiled as the others had, but neither had he told Louis not to call him that. Some of the other young men in town called him "Big Joe" but Louis and only Louis called him "King." Philip, of course, called him Joseph, as his parents did, and with the same deference he showed to their father.

One of Joseph's first attempts at influencing the family business was to persuade his father to open a new bank. The family had been dealing with loans, mortgages, and collections for so long that in the end it only made sense to open a regional bank. The bank was to be called Miners Bank of McAdoo. James was able to influence his father to assign him as the president at the new bank. The town of McAdoo was a larger town and was on the main road between Hazleton and Tamaqua so it was a focal point for the miners. The new granite bank building at the intersection of the road leading to Kelayres soon became a cornerstone in the community.

CHAPTER 7

THE NEW CENTURY

*T*he new century was turning out to be everything the Brunos hoped it would be. The family was well on their way to controlling—or at least having a large interest in—everything worthwhile in both the little mountain town of Kelayres and northeastern Pennsylvania. Their influence extended to the schools, local government, the banks, real estate endeavors, the mine, the railroad, gambling, liquor, and prostitution. The Brunos had strength in numbers: three brothers and now several fine sons and daughters growing up, marrying and bringing more sons and daughters into the family and its businesses.

The new century was good for the town of Kelayres, too, as well as for the entire region. The demand for coal was high, and most of the time the miners were working and earning enough money for a good life. The small businesses in town were doing well because the mine was successful. School attendance was rising now that child labor laws were being implemented.

On the whole life was good, but times had remained hard for some. In such cases, the Brunos took firewood, food, clothes, and shoes to the families. If a man died in the mine, the Brunos took care of his wife and children, help her find work, and organize the neighbors to help care for her home and children. Because there was a Bruno brother at the bank, the family could pay her rent or mortgage until she got on her feet again.

Frank and James still remembered their own lives in Italy where class and education meant everything and everyday life could be difficult. The men acknowledged the importance of respecting others, individually and culturally. They encouraged the people of different nationalities to keep their traditions and celebrate their holidays and festivals, while at the same time encouraging everyone to work together in harmony. In addition, protecting their children from the ugliness of life was of the utmost importance to them. The men wanted a good life, not just for their own children, but for all the children of the town.

The Bruno family justified their types of businesses by telling themselves that people would engage in such activities anyway, and if someone provided the amusements locally, then participants would not have to travel to distant towns, down dangerous mountain roads, or to cities where crime flourished. And, they were careful to point out that the money was reinvested in the town. The profits stayed local because the business owners were local and the family employed people from the village and the surrounding areas.

Sometimes, on cold winter nights, locked behind thigh-high drifts of snow, James would sit in front of the coal stove, reading his paper, sipping his Chianti, and wishing he were beneath the bright lights of New York City, or Philadelphia, or even Pittsburgh. When compared to the streets of those cities, where even on a cold snowy night there would be restaurants and saloons with steaming windows, spicy scents, good tastes, soothing liquors and friendly faces. Yes, life was slow in this little town.

Then James would remember why he was there: he wanted the prestige of being part of the ruling family of a town, an entire region. He realized that their family's fortunes had grown easily in this small town when it would have taken generations in Philadelphia, New York City and other big cities. The footprints of his powerful family were now cast in the coal-stained snow of Pennsylvania. Why bother to look elsewhere?

Later on the same evening, Marie would finish in the kitchen and come and sit by his side, taking his hand in hers. James would look into her clear, Mediterranean blue eyes and the rest of the world would vanish and all that would matter was this warm room, the children sleeping upstairs, and Mr. and Mrs. James Biaggio Bruno.

As his nonna had said many times, "As you walk through the forest you will always see a bigger, better stick to use as a hiking stick, but keep the one with which you feel the most secure, which will probably be the first since it is in your hands the longest. This makes the grip familiar and the stick more useful as time goes on."

Joseph and Cecilia's first child, the first grandson, was born in 1901, and christened *James* after his grandfather. Little Jimmy was the apple of his nonno's eye who would have carried him everywhere if his mama would have let him.

"Papa James," she said, "I know you love him, and I know he loves you, but he's just a baby. He needs his sleep. He's too small for so much excitement."

Cecilia was very protective of her young son. He was her firstborn, a treasure, and she wanted to keep him with her as much as possible and for as long as possible. James nodded at Cecilia's words, but he knew little Jimmy was like his grandpa and wanted to be in the middle of things.

James remembered his own nonno, the man who had shaped his childhood and who had encouraged him to start a new life in America. James found it incredible to realize that now he was the nonno.

In 1904-1905, respectfully, Frank and James each turned fifty years old. On the Fourth of July, midway between their two birthdays, the growing family gathered to celebrate the birth of the nation and half a century of Bruno determination and success.

The three brothers lolled under the shade of a big catalpa tree in the village park, sipping tall, cool drinks, and relaxing after a delicious feast. Frank squinted his eyes as he looked at the nearby mountain, standing tall and proud in the hot July sun.

"Ah, I don't know. I'm tired, James, I want a rest. I deserve a rest!"

"Frankie, Frankie, yes, you deserve a rest, but not yet, not yet! You're too young to give up! We're just getting good, Frank, you and me, we're in the prime of our lives!"

Peter chuckled and said, "James, when were you ever not in the prime of your life?"

James nodded, smiling as he said, "Well, yes, you're right there, little brother."

James suffered a laugh at his own expense but the dreaded subject of growing old and quitting was quickly forgotten.

"Father, I am tired of working in the colliery. I have had to wake up each morning to face that grimy filth while I watch you and my uncles, with your positions of respect, working in the town, so I have decided to run for office myself." Joseph spoke with such an air of authority and an attitude of persuasiveness that James knew it was only a matter of time until his son would be the one to carry on the family dreams.

"Joseph, my son, you are now so much like I was when your uncle and I came to America. You have my will, my hunger for more, my keen sense of what is my right. *What is your right,* Joseph?"

James realized he was speaking to his son man-to-man for the first time. Joseph had been active in various aspects of the family business for some years and had shown his determination and strength several times. Now he was beginning to make his own decisions, without first consulting his father or his uncles.

James quickly realized that the destiny he had dreamed of years ago back in Calabria was now in the hands of his sons, especially those of Joseph, but Philip's, too. The young men were in their early twenties. They were beginning to get a sense of who they were, what they wanted, and most important, how to get it.

Joseph had done as his father and uncles had told him, with some resistance, but James saw that time was now past. And none too soon, either. Though still not an old man, James was feeling the weight of the burdens of his life. He was still a vital man, as strong and wiry as in his youth, but something was missing now, a spark, a desire to accomplish everything. He remembered having chided Frank just a few years earlier about wanting to retire, and smiled. But it was true, he had worked hard and now he wanted a rest. So James began cutting back on his own responsibilities and handing them over to his sons.

A few years later the Bruno family celebrated Louis's graduation from law school.

"Now we have one of our own!" Frank shouted, pounding his son on the back.

Joseph was a bit envious of his cousin, but at the same time felt pleased that he had not spent time in school away from the action of the family business. He was now in line to be in charge, although he was already practically running the businesses himself. Uncle Peter was still working, but he had never considered himself the leader. He was quite willing to let his nephew take over the reins.

Nor did Louis challenge Joseph for the leadership position. He had made that decision as a boy; give Joe the limelight and he would stay in the background as a wise advisor. He was content to work in his office, studying the legal aspects of the business and keeping his hands clean. In the meantime, Joseph, always keeping in mind his own political ambitions, decided to become a bona fide United States citizen. Having been born in Italy, he had to renounce allegiance to Victor Emanuel II and did so in 1905. In 1907, Joseph, his brother Philip and his cousin Louis, each ran for offices in the Republican Party similar to those held by their fathers. As each of the elder Bruno men—Frank, James and Peter—grew grayer and less interested in politics, they began to step aside to let the new generation of American-raised Bruno boys take over the businesses they had built.

"Cecilia! We did it! We won!" Joseph called to his wife. "I am a director of the county schools"

"My Cecilia," Joseph continued. "Do you know what this means? All the hard work that papa and I have done over the years will continue. Philip as newly elected tax assessor, and Cousin Louis and I as school directors—we will all carry on. Our name Bruno will be looked upon as a name of distinction in this county, and no one will ever disrespect our heritage."

Cecilia ran to Joseph's outstretched arms, saying, "Joseph James Bruno, I am so proud of you!"

The 1907 election signaled the new era in the Bruno family legacy. With the three younger generation boys sworn into electoral positions, the official change of the guard could take place. So it was a time to celebrate.

Cecilia stepped back and clasped her hands together. "I will make the best sauce you ever tasted, and tonight we will celebrate! Hurry; go tell Phil and Louis to bring their wives, while I prepare a banquet to remember!"

"Why do you even bother to take an interest in them?" Joseph's new acquaintance said. "They would slit your throat as soon as you turned your back." Before he replied, Joseph offered a cigar to the man, a recent arrival from Calabria, and an even more recent suitor to one of Joseph's sisters.

"That is why you must never turn your back on your own kind," Joseph explained. "Always help them and never treat them as if they do not matter."

Joseph paused to light the cigars, then continued, "When my father first came here, he helped anyone who needed it. He said if he did not help someone, then he could not consider that person to be an ally or loyal friend. He taught me never to alienate prospective allies." The other man nodded, understanding the wisdom of Joseph's words. How much better to have allies than enemies, and how simple to make friends of them.

Retirement was hard for James Bruno. For him to let others have control, even if it was his own kin, was very difficult.

So he still dressed in his suit and tie every morning, ate his breakfast, donned his hat and walked to the center of town. He would visit the hall, the offices of his sons and his nephew.

But as the months slipped by, his family noticed that James moved ever more slowly, starting out later and later in the day, until some days he did not go out at all. He just sat in his big chair in the living room, or on the front porch, looking out at the Immaculate Conception Italian Church and the gardens.

One day in 1911, James Biaggio Bruno walked for the last time through the streets of the beautiful town he had helped found and build—the culmination of a dream dreamed in a small crowded village in southern Italy many years before. James and his brothers had worked tirelessly to make that dream, their dream, a reality. Now their town stood proudly in the mountains of Pennsylvania filled with the many descendants of that strong Italian family.

A grand ceremony and funeral service marked the passing of James Biaggio Bruno. People from the entire region turned out to honor such an eminent citizen of the town of Kelayres. Many had been touched by James' influence and generosity. They came one last time to pay their respects.to the man who had provided good lives for them and now would rest in the churchyard of the church he had built.

"Cecilia, my dear, we need a home, a fine big home, for our family," Joseph said one day. "Right in the center of town. A home that says who the Brunos are."

Joseph watched as Cecilia moved around the cramped room, first dressing Jimmy, now a toddler; then bending over baby Antoinette, just waking in her makeshift bed of pillows piled on top of her parents' large bed. Antoinette Marie had been born that year and named after her grandmother. She was a wonderful baby who tried anything and ventured anywhere.

"Yes, Joseph, we certainly do need more room. A house, yes, a house of our own."

Joseph and Cecilia and their children lived on the upstairs floor of Marie Antonia's home. They had two children and another one on the way and it was imperative that they have their own place. One, because they needed more room, and two, because they had to carry everything up and down the stairs, including the children.

"I would like to be in town, near the church. That would be so nice."

"We own land around the church. Which lot do you think you'd like best?"

"Your mama has told me of how the house in Sicily where she grew up was right across the street from the church and when the church door was open they could see the altar from their porch. And all her brothers became priests!"

"Would you like that? To be able to see the altar from your porch? And to have all your sons become priests?"

Cecilia laughed and said, "I don't think their papa would like them to become priests. He wants them in his business!"

Joseph smiled, nodding at his wife and wondering how he would feel if young Jimmy wanted to become a priest. It was a high honor, to have a son become a priest, but Cecilia was right— he wanted Jimmy working with him someday.

Joseph and Cecilia built a fine brick bungalow, the only brick home in Kelayres. The two-story house boasted a peaked roof, four big dormer rooms upstairs and plenty of storage as Cecilia had demanded. They had a porch on which to sit and enjoy a fine summer evening. And from the front door, when the church door was open, they could see the altar. The new home was valued at twice the cost of the next most expensive house in the area.

Joseph and Cecilia's new home was in the lot next to Joseph's childhood home. The pool hall was next door on the backside of the lot, bordering the alley. A brick wall built around the two homes lined the streets. The wall had fine Italian wrought iron gates that led into the property. When compared to the surrounding more modest homes, the brick wall and gates gave the large half-block of family residences the air of an estate. To some who disliked the family, the buildings seemed ostentatious and reminded them of a fortress.

Marie Antonia Abbaté Bruno was delighted with her son's new home. She helped the family celebrate, preparing her wonderful sauce and pasta, holding her grandchildren, sipping a bit of the dark Italian wine that flowed freely. But tears came to her eyes as she thought of her beloved James who was no longer with the family.

Joseph and Cecilia prepared a downstairs room for Marie Antonia in their new home which kept her in the midst of the family, cooking, helping with the shopping and tending the children. Antoinette Marie was ten that same year and having been named after her grandmother bore a wonderful likeness to her. She got into everything and had an opinion on everything. The family called her Nettie, short for Antoinette, but also because she needed to be put in a net to keep track of her whereabouts.

Life was peaceful and quiet in the early years of the new century. Men were occupied with business and industry, women with their homes and children, children with school and play. But as the century grew into its teens, a storm cloud grew over Europe that cast a shadow over the entire world. Though America's president, Woodrow Wilson, kept his country out of the war as long as he could, the United States eventually went to the aid of her allies.

The day, April 6, 1917, that President Wilson announced that America would join the war, Cecilia and the other Bruno women were in their big kitchen preparing the Sunday meal.

"Thank God our babies are too young to go!" Louis's wife exclaimed.

"Aiee! And our husbands too old!" said Philip's.

Everyone nodded and looked into one another's eyes with both fear and relief. Many women in the town and the country would not be so blessed, and these women all prayed for the safe return of all the men and boys who would go to war.

"But Mama, I want to do something important like the boys! Why do the boys always get to do the exciting things, the important things? It's not fair!"

"Antoinette, my dear one, what we do, what women do, is important, really more important than what the men do.

We make the home, the food, the babies. We keep the fires burning for the men to come home to after their wars. Think of that. Could the world survive without what we do? No. Could the world survive without wars? Yes."

Cecilia paused from folding the laundry to look at her daughter.

"Men worry about what is their purpose, why are they alive, how will the world remember them. But a woman, she holds her little child for as long as she can and her love is how the world remembers her. And maybe someday women will be remembered for being president, for inventing a machine, for writing a book. Yes, I can see that. But will a man be remembered for loving his child?"

"Oh, yes, Mama. Papa loves me!"

Her mother smiled and pulled her daughter close.

"Yes, love, yes, you remember that. Always remember that your papa loves you."

Certainly, Joseph doted over his little Nettie, the apple of his eye. He could tell from the first days that she was a force to be reckoned with. He was proud of her instincts to search out and control situations even as a toddler.

The war years were a boom time for the coal mining industry area of Pennsylvania, as well as for other industrial areas. The mines ran day and night. Many of the town's men had gone to fight so those who were left had to watch out for the women and children, the old and infirm. The Brunos helped as much as they could, keeping the children in shoes and coats, providing Christmas turkeys and gifts for families with little money. Finally the war came to an end.

The economy continued to expand after the war with the introduction of more industry. All the inventions used in the war were being converted to peacetime use—all kinds of vehicles, airplanes, assembly line production, automation of all kinds. At first the businesses all demanded coal, the hard coal supplied by the mines of Kelayres and neighboring mines. But when the businesses began to want soft coal, then fuel oil, a shadow of fear crept into the minds of the people in the mountains of

Pennsylvania who wondered what they would do if the world no longer needed their coal.

Now that the women of the country had their men home from the war, many women who before the war had vigorously spoken of their disgust with vices, once again took up the cause. Their voices reached a new high. The Women's Christian Temperance League flourished throughout the land, fighting with a zeal no less than that with which their men had fought the enemy in the trenches of Europe. Alcohol, gambling, prostitution—all the scourges of mankind were attacked by the high-minded women. The coal-mining region of eastern Pennsylvania was no exception and parades and marches by the zealous women became a common daily occurrence.

"Dizzy ol' dames. Damn, one of 'em is gonna get hurt out there and then we'll really be up the creek," Phil looked out the window of the hall at the group of women gathered outside, shouting and waving hand-painted placards emblazoned with phrases such as, "Demon alcohol!" and "Save our men from the devil!"

"Maybe we should invite them in for a little nip," Joseph joked as he sat down at the bar. The occupants of the saloon all laughed, a sorely needed bit of comic relief. Those "dizzy ol' dames" more often than not included their wives, mothers, or worse, mothers-in-law. If a man were seen leaving the hall, there would be hell to pay when he got home. But the men could always depend on Joe to leave the cellar door open so they could exit through the basement to the adjoining alley.

"What if they do succeed? It sure looks like they're getting those fool congressmen on their side. What're those guys thinking?" Phil pointed to the headlines of the paper Joseph had dropped on the counter.

The bartender slid a mug to Joseph, who said, "Well, it seems to me that, even if they make it illegal, alcohol isn't just going to disappear. And you can bet your bottom dollar that men are still going to want to drink it. So, you've got the liquor and you've got the men to drink it ..."

"And the women!" interrupted one of the streetwalkers who was an afternoon regular.

"You just need someone to provide a place in which to drink it," Joseph finished his little speech with a flourish of his overflowing mug, as if to say, "Don't worry folks, the Brunos will take care of you."

"What *are* we going to do about Prohibition, Joe?" Phil asked, his broad face lined with concern.

"I think it will be one of the best things to happen to the Bruno businesses. What do you think, Louis?" Joseph asked his cousin.

"I agree. Congress couldn't give us a better gift than to outlaw alcohol. Prices will skyrocket. People who didn't care one way or another before will suddenly want drinks. They'll want to know what's so special about this stuff that it takes an act of Congress to deal with it."

Joseph laughed and nodded his head. "And the Brunos will be here, ready and waiting to serve their community, as always," Louis added.

"You two are always one step ahead," Phil said, proudly. "We're just one hell of a team, aren't we, boys?"

The three raised their glasses in a toast to even greater Bruno success.

Louis had called it on Prohibition. In a matter of days after the 18th Amendment was passed by Congress in January 1919, legal saloons began closing and more than twice as many illegal establishments generated by the public's desire for drink and hiding behind various names—speakeasies, blind pigs, beer flats, shock houses—sprang up like wild mushrooms across the country.

The Brunos offered a tall cold one to anyone who came around with a bill or coin in hand. The basement, the pool hall, the dance hall—any place with a back room and a door that locked was a place to sell a glass of liquor. Cecilia even sold it on occasion from the kitchen cupboard when regulars would tap on her window while she was cooking a meal or rolling meatballs. That was just one more jewel in the Bruno crown that glittered and gleamed in the early years of the 20th century. It looked as if they were doing everything right, and could do nothing wrong.

In addition, Joseph ran several brothels in various forms throughout the region. He usually had his pick of women, and Cecilia found herself looking the other way. She knew that she was not like Marie Antonia, who knew James ran brothels but had never let him go near one himself.

"But Papa, don't you think women have the right to vote?"

"Ah, my dear Antoinette. That's a dangerous subject for me. If I say no, your Mama will be upset with me. If I say yes, the men who work for me and vote for me will think I've gone soft in the head. You see what I mean?"

"But Papa, women have just as much right to do things as men do, including voting. Women certainly do just as much work as men, even if they don't get proper credit for it. What is that old saying? 'A man's work is from sun to sun, but a woman's work is never done!'"

"Little Nettie, listen to what your president says: 'Sensible and responsible women do not want to vote. The relative positions to be assumed by man and woman in the working out of our civilization were assigned long ago by a higher intelligence than ours.' And I quote." Louis read from the morning paper the statement made by President Grover Cleveland.

"Don't you be quoting that nonsense in my house, Louis Bruno," Cecilia brushed the paper to the floor as she began setting steaming dishes of pasta, baked ziti, and fresh bread on the table. "The president using God to further such a position! How dare he?"

"But, Cecilia, he's right," Phil said, not realizing that he might be taking his life in his hands. "The Bible says that God made woman from man. That right there says that women are less than men."

"Philip, if you want some of this pasta that this little incomplete woman has cooked you will stop talking such nonsense right now."

Louis stood up and took the heavy dish from Cecilia, stepping between her and his cousin. The smell of tomato sauce, fresh basil and garlic was so pungent, he did not want an argument over politics to begrudge him a tasty meal.

"We can't stop the tide. Women will get the right to vote regardless of what anyone thinks."

Louis was always ready to step in to smooth over a problem or to soothe ruffled feathers.

"Hurrah for women!" shouted Antoinette.

"Finish setting the table, my fine girl, or you won't get to vote for anything!"

On August 26, 1920 Congress passed the 19th Amendment granting citizens the right to vote regardless of their sex.

When a man was a *cosca* leader, or destined to become one, especially if he were the heir apparent, his life was not completely his own. On many occasions he was reminded of his duties and responsibilities and what rules he was required to follow.

While being a *cosca* leader offered many advantages, a man in such a position, though envied, was not free to make the choices an ordinary man could make. For example, who would be the right woman to stand by his side as the leader of a powerful organization? Who would be the one to bear his children and raise his family? Who would the family find acceptable? The high stakes of ignoring the rules and expectations were never worth the lives that might be lost or damaged if the wrong choices were to be made.

All the young men knew that plenty of women were available at the brothels above the pool halls. Or a man could procure a young woman from Italy with very little trouble and keep her in the city out of sight of the family. But rarely would a young man in such a position entertain the notion of marrying a woman unqualified to be a *cosca* leader's wife. For putting such a woman in a vulnerable position could have dire consequences. No one would come to know this better than Carmine, the first love of Jimmy Bruno's life.

Jimmy met Carmine at one of the local church festivals in the village. The Immaculate Conception Italian Church of Kelayres held many festivals during its holy year. But the largest, and the favorite not only of the church members but also of residents of the town and the neighboring areas, was the Saint Mauro's Day celebration. This celebration was the best week of the year in Kelayres, and everyone was in high spirits, and generous to boot.

At the beginning of the festival every year, the priest would tell the story of the village's patron saint: a priest who had been the founder of the Benedictine Order, St. Mauro was from La Bruce, Italy, and was the first disciple of St. Benedict.

But all of that was ancient history. The town needed a guiding spirit and St. Mauro was chosen. The Immaculate Conception Italian Church of Kelayres had begun its festival honoring the sainted man some years ago, and now all the villagers from surrounding areas would come to Kelayres to enjoy the wonderful, fun-filled festivities.

The main attraction of the festival was the parade. Families would line up and carry *cinti* or small candle houses to show their devotion to the saint of the church. Then a group of six of the proudest young boys in the village would carry the statue of the saint through the doors of the church, down the steps and into the intersection at Fourth Street and Center Street. As the parade progressed, the crowds would make their way to the statue and pin dollar bills to his robes. The church used the money to help the needy. The act of pinning dollar bills to the robes of the saint was to create a sense of giving one's cares and concerns over to Saint Mauro for his intercession.

As Jimmy Bruno was still in his late teens, he, too, pushed and wiggled his way to the front to pin dollar bills to the fluttering light blue robes of the saint. That was when he first saw Carmine. She was also working her way to the front of the crowd, but she had one solitary bill which she had been saving for this special occasion.

As the two bumped each other for a position at the statue, their eyes met and try as they might, they could not help staring at each other. Carmine had seen Jimmy before at the Palace in McAdoo, where she and her girlfriends had admired his Italian good looks. Jimmy was very handsome with his olive skin and coal black hair, a combination that many young ladies could not resist. Young as he was, he had already had many women, but he had never felt in such a state of euphoria as when he saw Carmine.

After what seemed like an eternity of looking into her eyes, Jimmy managed to say hello and introduce himself. Carmine then broke loose of her own trance and the two began to talk as they pinned their offerings onto the robe.

As they watched the statue of the saint proceed down the streets of the village, he seemed to be smiling on them. They walked together, forgetting the crowd that swarmed around them. They saw only each other. It was as if they were caught together in the current of a swift-running river spilling toward the lowest part of the valley.

When they reached the park where the festival was to begin, the crowd spread over the open field. Only when the fireworks exploded above them did they realize where they were. They laughed together and made plans to meet each night of the festival at that very spot.

After the festival, Jimmy and Carmine continued to meet as often as they could—three, four, sometimes five nights a week, in dance halls, at the Palace, walking or driving in his car. Carmine was working in a dress shop in Hazleton, while Jimmy was working for his father.

Jimmy had been wondering how he was going to introduce Carmine to his mother when one day his Uncle Phil took him aside.

"Say, Jim, that girl you're seeing, you're not getting too attached to her, now are you?"

"What do you mean, Uncle Phil? She's a great girl. I like her a lot."

"Well, I don't know, it's just that she don't seem like the kind of girl your mama and papa would want you to be seeing."

"That's my decision to make," Jimmy answered defensively. Uncle Phil shook his head as he watched Jimmy stomp off down the street.

"Carmine, I love you! Let's run down to Philly and get married!"

"Oh, Jimmy, I can't do that! Mama would have a fit!"

"Well, then when can we get married?"

"Let's go talk to Mama."

When the two young lovers met with Carmine's mother, she asked, "Have you talked to your parents about this, Mr. Bruno?"

"No, ma'am. I'm an adult. I can make my own decisions," Jimmy said emphatically.

Carmine's mother was not so sure. This boy was a Bruno, the son of the most powerful man in the Bruno family. She looked around at her home and the neighborhood where she and her daughter lived. She was sure her daughter would not measure up to the standards of that family in many ways. She was afraid of what the consequences might be if these two ran off to get married.

"Jimmy, James, I want you to go down to the city with me to do some business and meet some of my contacts while we are there," Joseph said to his son.

"For how long, Papa?"

"Oh, I don't know a few days, a week. Have you got anything else to do that's more important than learning about the family business? I thought you wanted to learn it. Was I wrong?" Joseph turned to look at his young son, then smiled.

"Well, I guess a young man's got lots of important things to do, right?"

"No, of course I want to go, Papa, it's just …."

"Yes, son?"

"Oh, well, nothing, nothing, Papa."

Later, when Jimmy and Carmine were together, Jimmy said, "Carmine, honey, I have to go to the city with Papa, but as soon as I get back we'll go to Philly and get married. I don't care what your mother says."

"Oh, Jimmy! I'll miss you so!"

"I'll miss you, too, Carmine. Tell you what—I'll get you a ring when I'm in the city!"

"I'd like to have a few words with you, ma'am. I need your help and I hope you will let me make you an offer."

The man with a pleasant smile approached Carmine's mother. He was no one she had ever seen before, but he did not act like a salesman, and he was very polite. He walked up the stairs to the porch, eyeing a front yard and veranda that needed sweeping and tidying.

"Yes? What is it?" she questioned as she looked at him through the broken screen on the front door.

"It's about your daughter," he said as he put his hand around a thick banded roll of what appeared to be twenty dollar bills.

Carmine's mother was hardly surprised; she had been expecting such a visit. She knew that her daughter was out of her league dating a Bruno boy. She knew it was a relationship doomed from that first chance gaze, one that should never have been pursued. So when Jimmy and his father returned from their trip to the city, Jimmy hurried to see Carmine at her home.

"I'm sorry, Mr. Bruno," the landlord said as he answered the door, "but Carmine and her mother left last week. I don't know where they went. They told me to forward their mail to a brother in Pittsburgh until they get settled wherever they were going."

A neighbor, sitting on her front porch rocking a baby grandson, nodded her head as if to say, "That's what happened."

"They didn't leave anything for me? No note, no letters?" Jimmy said, almost breaking down. "Please think, woman, she must have left something for me."

"No, they didn't leave nothing. Only a note with the month's rent, in cash mind you, fresh twenties!"

"Ah, Jimmy, I told you she wasn't the kind of girl for you. See, now, she's run out on you. It's just as well you didn't get too serious."

Jimmy just stared at his uncle, then he slowly turned and walked down the street to the park, the same park where the festival had been held earlier in the summer, where he'd spent that first beautiful day with Carmine. He looked back toward his uncle as he walked and sadly knew why Carmine was suddenly gone from his world.

Didn't get too serious? What a joke. Wherever it was that Carmine's mother had taken her, she had taken the best part of Jimmy Bruno with her—his heart.

Jimmy was never the same after that. He worked for his father, he did what he was told, but he did it without spirit, without ambition. Though he never mentioned Carmine or asked what had happened to her, he suspected his father had something to do with her leaving and he no longer trusted him. But the family connection was so deep inside him that he could not leave nor be openly disrespectful or rebellious.

Regarding Joseph's other children, Alfred never had an interest in business of any kind; he was content being a teacher and school principal. Ernie and Elveda were too young to care and kept busy with their toys and schooling.

Things were different, however, for Antoinette, Jimmy's sister. She was a good girl, always there for her mother, helping out with the younger children and the household chores, but also very close to her father. She listened to him as he talked about the business and helped out in the office, filing, typing papers, running errands, doing whatever was needed.

Antoinette was an attentive listener and made herself so useful that Joseph soon began to depend on her, to trust her and confide in her. She was her father's daughter and quite savvy about practical business dealings. Joseph often discussed his plans with her and sought her opinion on decisions. Nettie was his girl, and with Jimmy losing interest in the business, it seemed natural for her to take his place. Of course, neither of them revealed the extent of their relationship—it would not have been proper for a woman at that time to be active in the business or to have the leader of the *cosca* taking advice from a woman, and a young one at that. While the men talked things over with their wives, who often offered invaluable practical views of things, neither acknowledged such a relationship.

Joseph never allowed Antoinette to do anything illegal— that was the one thing the men in his business understood. Wives were not required to testify against their husbands, but he did not believe the same was true for daughters. If Cecilia knew what Joseph did behind the scenes she never divulged a word. Antoinette probably knew more than was good for her, but he figured that if she were never put in a compromising position she would be safe.

Antoinette fell in love with Edward Billig, if not exactly the boy next door, then the one down the street, a nice young man she knew from high school. Her parents both approved of him even though his family had come from Austria, not Italy. Joseph so loved his daughter that he just wanted her to be happy. He was not threatening to Papa, yet he was polite to Mama. Just days after her eighteenth birthday and graduation from high school, Antoinette Marie Bruno walked down the aisle of the Immaculate Conception Italian Church in Kelayres, a radiant bride, straight and proud, on her father's arm.

To the sound of much laughter at the reception, Joseph recalled his father's fanatical admiration of Guiseppe Garibaldi, the hero who helped Italy gain independence from Austria, the homeland of the young groom's parents. Joseph just wanted his daughter to be happy. But because his daughter meant so much to him, he would keep an eye on young Edward. If he was the man to make her excited about life, then it was right.

"Who would have guessed these two countries could be joined in matrimony? To peace and harmony!" Joseph raised his glass of prohibited red wine in a toast.

"To peace! To harmony!" the guests responded with vigor. Everyone was eager for a time of peace and prosperity and all too happy to forget the recent war.

Jimmy watched the festivities from the sidelines. Antoinette was grieved that he was so sad on her happy day, but she did not try to make him participate.

Once again, the times were good for all. Business was booming, the mines were going strong, the people of the region seemed to have plenty of money to spend on still-illegal liquor, gambling and visits to houses of ill repute. The leaders of the Bruno organization continued to delegate more and more tasks to lieutenants. Louis and Joseph made the decisions; the lieutenants passed the orders down to the appropriate soldiers. If enforcement was necessary, which became more and more seldom, Phil said a few words to the right man and the wheels turned smoothly again.

The three young men, Joseph, Philip and Louis, worked beautifully together, each serving an important function, each depending on the others, all moving together in harmony. Joe was a benevolent monarch, visiting those in need, bestowing gifts everywhere. Frequently several villagers would be in line in the hall on the second floor of the Bruno home waiting to talk to Joe. But only the highest in the organization got to see Joseph for business.

Though their business had always done well, the Roaring Twenties really made the Bruno family successful. Prohibition continued to fill their cups to overflowing. People were dancing in the streets and drinking more than ever. When a call came to the Brunos that someone was thirsty, that call was answered. Saloons were operating 24 hours a day, seven days a week, and paying big money to the Brunos for protection. The family had developed a chain of houses of ill repute that stretched throughout several states, with girls being transported to and from New York, New Jersey, Delaware and Maryland. Slot machine operators alone paid as high as fifteen hundred dollars a month for protection.

The stock market was the biggest thing going; everyone wanted a piece of the action. Soon even the most timid members of the middle class were investing, and obliging brokers were offering people ways to invest that required very little actual money. Something for nothing was a bargain few could resist.

The family was deep into politics, wheeling and dealing at every turn. Joseph, or Big Joe, was the collector and fixer, taking money from one hand and slipping it into another, with a sizable portion being slipped into his own pocket during the transition. Joseph was also the head of the County Poor Board where he could help distribute to the poor people who helped support him.

In addition to all his other duties, Big Joe had become county detective, a position that enabled him to move freely in the back halls of justice. He had a pistol and the right to carry it. He had access to police records. He was firmly in control of the school system, which provided him with many opportunities to manipulate local Republican politics, offer contracts for services and appoint people to positions of power. Joseph had county commissioners in his pocket, as well as judges, numerous police officers, all manner of political small fry and bigwigs all the way up to the top of the Pennsylvania state government.

The school buses were still in the charge of the Bruno family, the next generation following in the footsteps of the previous, taking advantage of the widespread net of operations available to them. The Brunos continued to use the buses to run bootleg alcohol to honky-tonks, to shift the slots to various parts of the county, even on occasion running a rolling crap game right in the back of the bus, dodging from county line to county line, one mile and one minute ahead of the law.

On one such occasion, on the way to Hazleton, the bus was traveling heavy as it rolled up and around the mountain roads. It was filled not with children, but with a load of liquid sloshing back and forth in huge barrels jammed into the aisles.

"We need to make a side trip."

"Where to?"

"You're gonna love this—that little joint down by the creek."

"Huh? What creek?"

"The one with the funny name."

"Oh, you mean Hunky-dory creek."

"Yeah, they want a barrel over there."

"Oh, great. How do we get there?"

After finding the Hunky-dory speakeasy, the men got back just in time to the garage to unload and gas the bus for school.

♦ ♦ ♦

Then the bottom dropped out. The sky fell and not a few of the high and mighty jumped after it. The Stock Market Crash of 1929 was an unprecedented disaster to the economy of the United States destined to change the course of events in the world. The little town of Kelayres, Pennsylvania, and the large, extended Bruno family were no exception

CHAPTER 8

TROUBLES

Actually, fate dealt two blows to Kelayres, Pennsylvania. If the Great Depression was not already bad enough, the United States had continued to shift from using hard coal to soft coal and oil for fuel, virtually pulling the rug out from under the economy of the mining communities in the northeastern part of the state. As county detective Joe tried to curb the coal bootlegging that was now rampant in the area. While bootlegging was illegal, most people looked the other way. Men would mine coal from abandoned mines and sell it on the black market. Such behavior turned many people against Joe.

The Miner's Bank of McAdoo was just one of hundreds of banks forced to close its doors. But the effect on the community was not as bad as in other areas. The Brunos knew most of the people in the town who had mortgages and Joseph wanted to save families from losing their homes, so many of their loans were converted to personal loans. It was said that 75% of the mortgages in the village were loans made through Big Joe. With the loss of jobs, small businesses lost sales themselves and had to cut credit to their customers in order to make payments on their loans to the Brunos. Such activities added together to incite the villagers in the area against the family.

Both the garage and basement in Cecilia's home were packed with flour, beans, potatoes, apples, sugar, and other commodities. She was kept busy filling women's sacks with those necessities, with no expectation of repayment.

But because the family businesses were diversified and because they were involved in alcohol, gambling, and prostitution, prosperity stayed fairly level for the Brunos. And, of course, politics never went away. But the loan business was the one area where the family purse was hit hard. The towns-people could not easily pay back their loans when they had no jobs.

Over a bowl of Cecilia's best pasta and meatballs that would leave one singing of garlic, the men would plot their latest schemes. No one could be sure where another jackpot would appear, but it was important to cover as many bases as possible.

The family controlled the local whorehouses and the pool halls were all run with their authority or not at all. The schools had long been their playground, along with the banks, the local mines, vote selling, protection—you name it, they did it. But the time had come for the family to be serious. The men and their wives and children needed to become a part of the gentry, no longer simply aspire to it. They needed to put down roots in the real houses of power, to ride the crest of their wave of success to the very top. So they began planning how to catch the biggest fish yet, the Governor's mansion in Harrisburg, which would become vacant in the next election three years away.

"Joseph, dear, what is it? Aren't you feeling well?"

"It's nothing. I'm fine. Really, now, don't make a fuss."

But Joseph decided to stay at home that day instead of going out on his regular rounds.

"I'm just going to catch up on some reading, Cecilia. Maybe lie down for a bit."

Joseph looked so pale, Cecilia knew he was in pain. But she did not dare say anything. He was always so anxious about getting old, losing his power, his strength. For him to stay home, go to bed in the afternoon was unusual, to say the least.

Maybe, Cecilia thought, *she should just give Doctor DeMarco a call. She would invite him over, say it was just for some coffee and he could see Joseph. Then if he thought it necessary, he would talk to him. The doctor was a longtime friend and knew Joseph so well he would be able to see immediately if something was wrong.*

By 1932, the residents of northeastern Pennsylvania were leaving in droves, desperately looking for work, for income, wherever they could find it. Some actually left the United States to return to the countries from which they or their forebears had come. Those who had nowhere to go stayed, but there were so few jobs that many were unemployed, some not far from becoming homeless and others already out on the street. In his area, Joseph made sure people had somewhere to shelter.

President Hoover was desperately trying to stabilize the ship of state, demanding that congress balance the budget and trying to sell the idea of a federal sales tax. In January 1932, Congress passed legislation to stem the tide of drowning corporations and businesses. Some people were angry that Hoover would help corporations but not the unemployed. The depression was a difficult time and would have been a challenge for any leader, but Hoover's actions led to his downfall.

Franklin Delano Roosevelt had had power thrust on him in the governor's race in New York in 1928, and the same thing happened at the Democratic Convention of 1932. Too many candidates were splitting the votes, possibly leading to the nomination of a man who could not beat Hoover, so the powers-that-be worked behind the scenes to secure the nomination for Roosevelt.

One of Roosevelt's campaign promises was to repeal Prohibition.

"Well, that would be the end of that sweet deal," Philip said as the men sat listening to the radio.

"It won't matter to us, we still have the halls and the games and ... everything else," Joseph didn't complete his thought. He looked over at Louis who was frowning.

"What? Louis, what's wrong with you? You don't think that will hurt us, do you?"

"Well, it certainly won't help. It seems like everything is breaking down at once—the coal, the stock market, the Democrats getting elected and now repeal of prohibition. What next?"

"The Democrats have not gotten elected here and they're not going to," Joseph said firmly with much resolve. "That is one thing we are sure won't change."

Louis just nodded his head as he stared absently at the radio. The broadcast had turned to news of election matters. Locally, the Democrats were actually posing a thorny campaign for the school superintendent position. Many people who had been hurt so badly by the depression were looking for a change. When times become hard, people often forget who helped them get where they are, or where they came from.

The brothers were still helping the villagers. Many families held onto their homes under the cloud of repossession by the banks. The brothers, through Louis, devised ways for the families to keep them. While it meant they would have to pay interest and be beholden to the Brunos, the alternative was far worse. Louis, always the, cautious one, was constantly on the lookout for any help the family could give to others, perhaps to stave off what he seemed to feel was inevitable.

Joseph, for his part, made a habit of attending many of the local area events, such as softball games, to keep in touch with the community. Antoinette loved to go with him. She was always amazed that he knew every player by name. If the players mentioned in any way that their family was in need or if the teams needed uniforms, Joseph always gave from his own pocket.

One time Antoinette returned from college in Kutztown. She loved being around her papa, but she quickly saw how he had aged. She also knew how the hard times for the village were difficult for him. She knew that he felt the people were part of his family and it bothered him to see them hurting. She was sure this was part of his aging look and why he was so tired from his worries. Mama had said it was harder for Papa to get out each morning. Doctor DeMarco had come by a few times, "for coffee." He could not however get to the root of Papa's situation, other than he seemed preoccupied and stressed. *Small wonder,* Antoinette thought, *with all the multiplying problems in the village and the family businesses.*

The family persuaded Joseph to have some tests done and the results showed him to have a kidney problem, The illness was progressive and major symptom were fatigue and disorientation in the later stages of the condition which was known at that time as Bright's Disease.

Then, suddenly, on one horrible day, Louis was dead. He had been standing on a corner in McAdoo waiting to cross the main intersection near the saloon when a car approaching the corner appeared to lose control on the slippery mountain road. Louis was hit by the car, thrown some distance and pinned between the car and a light pole. He was rushed to the hospital in Hazleton with multiple injuries. In spite of all the efforts of the medical staff, Louis died within hours of head injuries. The driver was never found and the investigation resulted in a finding of accidental death. However, some were not so sure.

The entire Bruno clan was in shock. They were a close-knit family and Louis had been like a brother to Joseph, Philip and the others. Louis was buried with all the honor and ceremony due a *cosca* leader. The whole town turned out for the event— the Republican faction, anyway. But Louis's funeral was not the end of it. While he was a great loss to the family as a whole, to Joseph, already unwell, it was a deep sorrow that at times overwhelmed him.

"What does it matter, Joe? Louis is dead!" Phil cried

"It does matter! Can't you see they're out to get us? We're up here on top of the mountain, and they don't like it."

Cecilia knew better than to ask who "they" were or to encourage him in any way. She took his hand and said, "Come on, Joe, sit down and eat your dinner. You haven't eaten all day. Look, here's your favorite pasta, fettuccini carbonara— Antoinette made it for you—just like your mama used to make it. *Mangia*, Joseph, *mangia!*"

"You sound like Mama," he grumbled, but he sat down as instructed.

Cecilia smiled behind his back, knowing that he was paying her a compliment when he said she was like Marie Antonia, but she was worried all the same. He was becoming more and more upset and she feared for him.

"What do you mean, Joe?" his brother-in-law asked.

Cecilia flashed him a look—'Don't get him started!' but it was too late.

"It wasn't an accident! I don't believe that—Louis was too careful, too cautious."

"What do you think happened then?"

"I think someone did something—tampered with that car, purposely drove out of control toward him. It was a set up—I don't know how they did it, but I know they did!"

"Joseph ..." Cecilia quivered with the fear of what had been implied. She thought of her dearly loved husband and what this all meant. "*Jesu Cristo* my Savior." Everyone turned to her, saw the look of deep disturbance painted on her solemn face. Everyone present immediately felt a dark sense of danger looming, as if a bit of coal dust had gotten into the Bruno machinery.

Soon it seemed the wheels of the businesses were not turning as smoothly; but grinding, creaking, and an occasional squeal. The machine that had functioned so superbly for so long was breaking down.

The three men at the top had been like a scale, a delicate instrument. Joseph was in the middle, the fulcrum. Like two arms extending on either side, Louis was the brains and Philip the enforcer. They balanced each other and represented the whole family, the whole operation. But their perfect triangle had been destroyed and the two who were left were so used to the way things had been, they could not begin to envision how they would continue without that third arm, Louis. The scale was now finally tipping toward Philip, the enforcer. It had to be, it was a natural realignment. With the death of Louis leaning toward foul play, enforcement became the overriding preoccupation. With the death of Louis, Joseph had lost one confidant; but he gained, or rather, regained, another—his daughter, Antoinette.

Antoinette and her husband were living in rooms above a speakeasy in nearby McAdoo, and like most people they were trying to get by. Antoinette kept busy teaching at the Kelayres School and raising their two daughters. Though much of the time the two children were cared for by their *nonna*, Cecilia. Their apartment was too small and noisy from the bar below, and their mother was busy at school, so the girls preferred staying at Nonna's big house. Nettie had not had much time to help Joseph the way she used to, and both of them missed the connection. She was as active in the political party as she was allowed to be as a woman, but it helped that she was the boss's daughter.

One evening, after picking up the girls up from her mother's house, she came home late from a Republican Party meeting, Antoinette found the apartment dark, which was surprising as her husband should have been home hours earlier. Sighing and wondering where he was, she flipped the light switch in the bedroom as she unpinned her hat. The screech that followed nearly caused her to stab herself with the long pin.

"Oh, God! It's her!"

"Turn the damn light off!"

Antoinette did as she was told, numbly pinned her hat back in place, hurried the girls back into their coats and climbed back down the stairs. She was too tired and stunned to walk all the way back to her parents' house so she stepped just into the door of the speakeasy and asked the man there to telephone her father.

Joseph was there in five minutes to pick up his daughter and granddaughters and drive them back home to his own house. Then he kissed Antoinette and said, "Don't worry about a thing. I'll be right back."

Joseph drove back to McAdoo, stopped in the speakeasy long enough to beckon to two of his men, and climbed the steps to the apartment.

The girl was gone, but the red-faced husband was still trying to get into his pants.

"You have one hour to be out of town," Joseph said quietly. He normally would not have conducted such business himself, but this was a very personal matter. "And I don't ever want to see your face here again."

Antoinette and her daughters were reinstalled in the family home, and Antoinette became even more active in her father's business. The house was more like a lively home again. Ernest was away at boarding school at the well-respected military academy in Hershey, and when Elveda married, she had moved out to a home in downtown Hazleton.

The big house was once again full of life. Nettie's friends were always visiting her. And the hardwood floors echoed the children's laughter as they played and ran around through the large rooms,

"Mama? What's wrong with Papa?" Antoinette had passed her parents' room on her way downstairs and seen her father lying on the bed with the shades drawn at five in the afternoon.

"Well, he says it's nothing. That he's just tired. 'I'm an old man, Cecilia!' he shouts at me. But if anyone else even hints that he's old he shoots them right down!"

"What does Doctor DeMarco say? You told me he finally went into see him for an exam last week."

"It's something with his kidneys, nothing serious, but nothing he can do anything about. Joseph just needs to take care of himself, get enough rest, and eat right."

Antoinette frowned and said nothing, but she and her mother both had the same thought—that he should not continue to stay out all night, drinking God knew what with his cronies, traveling to New York and Philly all the time—and involving himself in other activities which neither would even think about, much less mention.

Antoinette decided at that moment that the time had come for her to be more deeply involved in her papa's businesses. There were few women strong enough to take on such matters, but she was one of the few. She also looked a little deeper into every detail so that she could understand more than her father allowed. Thus she learned in a very short time more than any of her brothers knew. Cecilia saw the look of concern on her daughter's face and couldn't stop her tears. Antoinette took her mother in her arms and held her close.

"Oh, Nettie! I am worried about him! He seems so ... I don't know, so sad, so distant! So unhappy, lost—something is terribly wrong. When you or Jimmy or Freddie looked like that when you were little I would have picked you up and carried you to Nonna's rocker and held you until you smiled again. But I can't do that with Joe. Dear Joseph. I worry about him so."

Joseph stood in the stairway and listened to his wife weeping, his daughter consoling her. He turned and climbed quietly back up the stairs to his office and closed the door. He reached for the light but stopped and sat down in the near dark.

What had his wife said about him? That he was sad. Yes, that was it. Sad. That summed it up, he thought. He sometimes wondered why he should even get out of bed. What was happening to him? He wondered if Louis had not gotten the best deal after all—dying quickly, painlessly, and missing all this mess, all these hard times, all these problems.

Perhaps it was time to turn the business over to Jimmy and Fred, with Antoinette helping, of course. Perhaps he himself was over the hill, too old to be trying to do everything himself, especially now, without Louis's help.

Why did he feel this way? Joseph wondered. *Was it just because he was getting old? He denied loudly that anything was wrong, when anyone else mentioned his age, but he worried about it in private. Maybe he needed a trip to the city, see his old friends, take in a show, tour the town; maybe see a lady or two.*

That's it, that's just what the doctor ordered, Joseph thought as he reached for the light pull. At the same moment he caught a whiff of garlic bread that had been slipped under the door and he breathed deeply. *Yes! Exactly what the doctor ordered!*

On a cold winter morning in 1932, the main school in Kelayres burned down, probably from the coal furnace malfunctioning, although there were those who suggested the fire might have been arson. The same people claimed that the Bruno family would stand to make considerable profit from the building of a new school by awarding contracts and providing building supplies. Others said that the Democrats did it to set up the Bruno family and to put questions in the minds of the voters.

Whatever the reason for its destruction, the fact was that the school had to be rebuilt. The board was divided as to who should have control of the contracts for the rebuilding of the school: the coal company or the Bruno family. In the end the Bruno family prevailed, and they awarded the contracts and controlled the money for materials and supplies and everything else that was needed.

The new school had fifteen classrooms and was made of brick, like its predecessor. The school board named the new school the Bruno School, although no vote was ever recorded. In 1933 the school opened with a large ceremony, and the main event was the unveiling of the granite lintel over the front entrance on which the words "Bruno School" had been carved in big, bold letters.

The Democrats had not had a political foothold in Carbon or Schuylkill Counties for years, not with the Bruno family in firm control of the Republican Party since the early twenties. Nor had a Democrat even considered placing a serious bid for any of the local elected offices. In fact, Democrats had not won a statewide election since the Civil War. The Republican's secret was in the control of the county commissioners and the election boards. A few dollars here and there at the beginning of an election period never hurt.

Some men who had been Republicans and who had fought unsuccessfully against the Bruno power structure from within the party, had given up and changed parties. They were now registered as Democrats, prepared to vote as Democrats and to run for office as Democrats.

Because of the economic depression that held the whole country in its grip, people across the land were ready to blame their problems on those who had been in office when the trouble began, the Republicans. People were completely willing to forget the years of unparalleled prosperity they had enjoyed, times during which those same men had been in office.

In fact, they were inclined to boot them out of office at the first opportunity.

One of the families who changed parties was a Sicilian family. They had come to the town sometime after the Bruno brothers, and at some point something happened to divide the two families. Joseph never really knew the whole story, but the animosity had grown until it had become almost a feud. Typically no love was lost between Italians and Sicilians, but Joseph's mother had been Sicilian, so he knew that that alone was not the cause. In fact there were rumors that she was a distant cousin.

At one point, the other family changed the spelling of its name, not much, a few letters rearranged, until now it looked Irish. At first Joseph thought it was a mistake but when he saw it printed again in the same fashion, he was surprised the family would do such a thing. He, Joseph, would never think of giving up his heritage and family name, especially after all they had accomplished. Although he knew that many families did so to "Americanize" themselves.

"That same guy made a smart comment to me today, like he was trying to pick a fight," Fred told his father as they sat down in Joseph's office, preparing to go over the week's receipts.

"I've always said, 'You must never turn your back on your kind.' This is what happens if you do," Joseph said sadly. "A fine Sicilian family—Sicilian! Now they've got this name that looks like Irish! Irish! I mean, I know some of our good friends are Irish, but to change a Sicilian name so it looks Irish? All because we didn't let them into our organization?"

"What did happen, Papa? Why do they hate us so much?"

"I don't know, son, I don't know."

The Bruno family had controlled the school board for over twenty years, and had played an active role for another ten or more before that. In recent years, others had tried to oppose them, but with little success. In 1932, when several town members began to bolster the Democratic Party in an attempt to defeat the Republican Party and the Bruno family, the situation was not taken seriously. It was clear that defeating the Brunos would not be an easy task, and from that point on the battle progressed, with both sides taking inappropriate actions.

On the Bruno side was Joseph's brother Philip, who had been reelected as the tax assessor and tax collector for the county. In that position Philip had the power to assess or not assess, collect or not collect taxes. At that time and place, a person could not vote unless he or she had been assessed taxes and had paid those taxes in full by the election deadlines. Many people claimed that they were willing to pay their taxes but were never assessed or had been unable to pay them for other reasons. One Democrat actually ran for office, but because he had not paid his taxes on time, not only could he not vote, but he also became ineligible as a candidate.

In addition, Joseph was the justice of the peace in the county and had control over voter registration. One candidate in the school board election was listed in the wrong column as a Republican although he was running as a Democratic candidate. Thus he could not even vote for himself as he was not a registered party member.

As the depression deepened, jobs grew more and more scarce. Franklin Roosevelt was elected to the presidency in 1932, bringing the Democrats back into the White House for the first time since Woodrow Wilson. But during the lame duck interval between Roosevelt's election and when he took office, the country sank into a deeper hole.

"The only thing we have to fear is fear itself," Roosevelt told his country in his inauguration speech. But too many in the country at that time were already fearing hunger and homelessness.

The thought of all the pain and suffering that her fellow villagers were forced to endure troubled Cecilia deeply. She often gave the mothers from the town flour from the garage storage bins, or vegetables from the garden to help them feed their families. Many times, without Joseph's knowledge, she would slip them a few coins to go to Lotsie's grocery store for essential items. She thought Joseph would be proud of her efforts, but she knew he would be angry if they were mentioned.

In Kelayres, the Democrats were starting to win over more and more voters. At the same time, the Republicans were struggling to come up with new ideas to help voters reconsider their party affiliation. For example, a letter was sent out to voters throughout the county stating that the coal companies which employed many of the men eligible to vote was backing the Republican Party and the Republican candidates for the election. No one ever figured out where this letter actually originated, as the coal companies claimed they had no hand in it.

Joseph sat at his desk, alone in his office. He looked out the window from the second-floor dormer window behind him. The doors were wide open at the church across the street, and he could hear the organist Mary practicing for mass. He was feeling somewhat better. The organ music soothed him and his recent little trip to the city had been a success. But he was still tired and found himself sleeping more and eating less.

Joseph thought about the Democrats and the business and wondered what he should do, wondered what Louis would have said they should do. He thought of Fred, of confiding in him. Fred was always there at his beck and call, would do anything for his father. And young Frank, Louis's son, had turned to Joseph for guidance now that his own father was gone. Frank was well on his way to becoming a fine lawyer himself, but he had not recovered from the shock of losing his father so suddenly, so early.

Then Joseph thought of Jimmy, his oldest son, his pride and joy. Joseph was disappointed that he showed so little ambition, so little interest in the business. Granted, he was obedient, and good at what he did but he never put himself out. What had happened to him? When did he change? Why did he change? Did it have anything to do with that girl? Surely not!

In those days, Antoinette was Joseph's saving grace. She was always cheerful and supportive, always did everything he asked her to do. More often than not, she anticipated what he would want her to do next. All this she did and taught her class at school and took care of her family. A man is certainly lucky to have such a daughter, Joseph thought, but sometimes he wished she had been a son.

Joseph knew he needed to let the next generation take over, and soon. Phil was anxious to retire, to take his well-deserved rest. Joseph sometimes thought that it would be nice to take a rest, take Cecilia back to Italy, to Sicily, really travel through the country, take the time to get to know it, enjoy it.

But every time he had such a thought, he jumped up and headed for the door, for the car, to drive around the town, his town, check on the businesses and visit his people. No, not yet, not just yet. He was certainly not so old a horse as to be ready for pasture!

On May 3, 1933, the Democrats held an open-air meeting on the eastern end of the county at which some men spoke about the election and the Bruno family's control over the school board and other offices in the county. After that, once a week or so, the Democrats held open-air meetings where all passersby, including children, could hear the ranting about how the Bruno corruption with its unfair control was destroying their lives. As the weeks passed, the events began to draw more people.

The effects of the great Depression were becoming more noticeable, and many of the people that happened upon the meetings were swept into the atmosphere of rebellion the gatherings generated. Some of the same people owed everything they had to the Bruno family. Houses had been built with Bruno money and mortgages arranged through the Bruno Miners Bank. Sometime later when the Bruno Miners Bank reopened as the National Bank of McAdoo, of which Joseph and his son Jimmy were board members, many of the mortgages were in default due to high unemployment in the area, but the delinquencies were overlooked while the Brunos were in control.

In many cases the Brunos had mortgaged the properties personally, allowing the families to remain in their house and make payments either directly to the Brunos or to the Bruno-run bank. In that way families could keep their homes, while the Bruno family held the notes. Such loans were made to those people who had always been friends and supporters of the family.

As more mines closed and the school board election approached in November of 1933, tension in the town had grown higher. As the open-air meetings of the Democrats grew larger, louder, and uglier, the people who attended them became more outspoken in their daily lives, too. Children would boo Bruno family members in town, and on several occasions Joseph's wife, Cecilia, was verbally assaulted. At Lotsie's grocery or Saladago's Drug Store, Cecilia would hear muffled, whispered, hateful remarks about her husband or family members.

Other Bruno family members also felt afraid as they went about the county on regular business. Some days the grandchildren did not go to school, and the wives sent servants for groceries or to pick up the mail. Antoinette actually began carrying a billy club in her purse. Other Bruno women took clubs with them even to the church across the street. The clubs were placed under the pews or right beside the Psalm books as they prayed. The deeper the battle lines were drawn, the more noticeable and ugly the remarks and behavior became.

As time passed, Joseph became more and more concerned about the outdoor meetings the Democrats were holding. Their nearest neighbor was one of the ringleaders and often had a noisy, boisterous crew gathered on his own front porch. The Democrats began gathering in one place, then walking to another, often past the Bruno homes and businesses. The women were becoming more and more frightened not only when they had to go out, but inside their own homes as well.

Obtaining firearms wasn't difficult for someone in Joseph's position. After all, he was a county detective. He had several locked away in case of emergency, but now he began to consider that option more seriously. He began to look into the types of guns available and to find places where he could purchase them. He could not believe that his life had reached the point when he would need to have a gun to defend his family and his home. Here! In Kelayres, the town the Bruno family built.

Joseph had his sons build a secret compartment under the staircase, right off the first floor landing, in a spot that was easily accessible to both the front door and the kitchen. The compartment was built under three of the steps. One step was hinged and when lifted up, two more steps would fold upward revealing the hidden guns. Another hiding place was constructed in the attic eaves off his bedroom. It was so well hidden that Cecilia would sometimes forget it was there and rearrange the furniture, thus blocking its entry.

Shortly before the election, the family celebrated Joseph's fiftieth birthday with a small party. They had been planning a big double celebration, just like the one they had had for Frank and James almost 30 years ago, but Louis would not now see his fiftieth year, his sudden death still haunting the family at every turn. Joseph's Uncle Frank had been ready to retire at fifty, but his father James had still been going strong. He had hung on for a few more years, then let his sons Joseph and Phil, and their cousin Louis take over. But though he had debated the issue, outwardly Joseph was showing no signs of handing over the reins. Since Louis died Joseph had begun taking Antoinette and Freddie into his confidence more and more, but he had not yet given them additional power.

The day of the 1933 school board election finally came. As the polls closed and the election results came in, election officials gathered in a tense atmosphere to count the votes. The head official counted the straight party ticket ballots first, each party separately. In that count the Republican candidates were ahead by several votes and the official nodded his head in Joseph's direction. This pleased Joseph—in the close election that was a good indication of the overall turnout. But then the officials counted the split party ballots and in the end it appeared that the Republican candidates had lost by about fifty votes.

Of course, Joseph challenged the count. The officials met and determined that the ballot box should be sealed and sent to Pottsville to be recounted at the Schuylkill County Courthouse. There, the judge opened the ballot box by cutting the tape with a letter opener on his desk, the ballots were removed and the counting began. Some of the ballots appeared to be votes cast for the Republicans but looked as if they had been changed one way or the other by erasing. After more than twelve hours the recount was over, the previous results successfully challenged, and the Republican candidates were declared to be the winners.

That was not the end of the election, however, as the battle for control of the county continued. The Democrats now contested the recount vote and demanded another, claiming the ballots had not been recounted fairly, that some ballots had the look of eraser marks and tampering, and a few others were found in a waste paper basket at one of the polling stations.

As a second demand for recount went before the courts, the anger and frustration at the election results spilled over into the community. Tempers were short everywhere, but especially at the school where several teachers were suspended for fighting in the halls, and parents pitched battles on the front steps. Officials closed the schools until people could cool off. Then the courts announced a verdict of widespread ballot tampering. The fighting escalated, with threats flying back and forth, causing officials to shut down the schools for months.

Then the Democrats made their next move—to smear the name of Joseph Bruno. They arranged for several teachers to complain to the school board that Joseph as school director had forced them to pay him fees and do illegal things to keep their jobs. One woman teacher claimed that he had even asked her if she would consider going out with him and other personal questions.

These accusations were so humiliating and embarrassing to the family that in January 1934 Joseph resigned his position on the school board rather than risk being subjected to more slander. He made one more move before he left office. He encouraged the board to name his son Fred as his successor, which it did, and subsequently elected him as head. That move caused further resentment on the part of the Democratic Party members who began calling for a new election.

Joseph had always been a good leader, but his long years of experience had been in the good times when he had a strong team surrounding him. Men like Louis who always figured out the right move at the right time. Things were now bad in so many ways, and his support system and chain of command was severely damaged. Joseph began having trouble making the day-to-day decisions.

Joseph was depending more and more on Antoinette and Freddie and always included Jimmy in discussions. But Jimmy rarely offered an opinion, simply agreeing with whatever the others said while showing little desire to help drive the operations.

"They can't do this to us. We are the Brunos!" Joseph slammed his fist into his hand as he stalked from one end of his office to the other for perhaps the hundredth time in the last hour. Things had been so good! What was happening?

Philip nodded his head mutely, his face puckered like a child who is about to cry.

"It's all Louis's fault," he said angrily. "He should have been more careful."

Joseph looked up at Philip's distraught face and felt his first twinge of doubt. How could they continue without his cousin Louis? Louis had always been there for him, to answer his questions, to find information, to debate the issues with him, to help him see the whole picture. Phil was a great brother, a big help, but it was not the same. He was not Louis.

Joseph sank into his desk chair, his head in his hands, and listened to the rain pouring down on the roof. *Well,* he thought, *at least that wasn't leaking.*

Finally, the court granted a contested election procedure. The hearing was scheduled to be held at the McAdoo firehouse, as the turnout would be large and that was the only place large enough to accommodate the crowd. Many teachers were questioned about the votes they had cast. Several claimed that they had been told how to vote or were given money for their votes. Some suggested that they were threatened with losing their teaching positions if they did not vote for Joseph Bruno's candidates.

One voter said she received ten dollars to vote Republican. One man, when asked why he let someone else mark his ballot, stated that the coal dust cinders from the street had gotten in his eyes, and even though Election Day was rainy and there would not have been any dust, he stuck to his story. Others testified that they had gone to church to ask the Lord to forgive them for voting the way they did, but they had been afraid of reprisals.

At the conclusion of the hearing, it was suggested that the two Republican candidates had lost the election. However, several of the election officials swore under oath that the ballots were in the same condition as when originally counted and had not been altered, that they had been sealed in public view after the first count on election night and not touched by anyone until the recount at the courthouse. The public hearing therefore resulted in a deadlocked decision. The contested election would have to be decided by the courts—a process which could go on indefinitely. This caused a great deal of turmoil, emotion, and anger on both sides.

After several weeks with no decision forthcoming, the Democrats took matters into their own hands. They picketed the school and refused to let the teachers enter. The school remained closed for a few weeks. Joseph refused to be bullied and felt the teachers were not at fault for the closure and therefore continued to pay them during this period. That angered many of the opposition as they viewed the teachers as political backers being paid for their support. In these hard times when many had no jobs, the Democrats argued, why should these Republicans get a salary for not teaching?

Joseph Bruno continued to help people in the ways he had learned from his father and uncles, but it was becoming a strain for him to be gracious. More people than ever before came to him for help and he was hard pressed to offer support. Others were attacking him and his family, blaming them for the troubles of the town. But the family organization itself was still standing strong. Most of the people who worked for them continued to believe and trust in them. Money was still coming in from the

various parts of the business and most of their people continued
to function in their jobs.

Much was at stake in the community for the Brunos, not just
Joseph's political career. He no longer had the power of his key
function in the county as school board president having earlier
resigned that position. It was not just a matter of this person or
that deciding he wanted a say in how his grandchildren's school
was run. The school board was a powerful piece of the Bruno
business puzzle and the family needed to be deeply entrenched
in the entire school system. Three schools were now under the
supervision of the board which controlled an extensive budget
and had the power to make many appointments so the family had
to keep control of it. At that point, Joseph was still the truant
officer and custodian of the school buses. Cecilia, his wife, held
three positions—an office clerk, a truant officer and in charge of
school maintenance. His son Fred was the school board president
as well as the bus driver. Joseph's brother Philip was in charge
of the school buildings and his daughter Antoinette and son
Jimmy were teachers, as were several nieces and nephews. The
family knew that the future of their business interests was partly
dependent on their positions of authority in the community.

"Ah, Joseph, what has happened to our life? Where is the
sweetness we had when we first married? Do you remember that,
Joseph?"

"Yes, yes, Cecilia, I remember. I remember the first time I saw
you, when I told myself you were the one for me and would be
my wife. Life will be better again soon, I promise you. We just
need to wait for all this election nonsense to blow over, for things
to settle down again, and then all will be fine, just wait and see.
We'll be back on the top of the mountain where we belong."

Joseph stood tall and proud before her, the way he always did,
as if he never had a doubt in the world of his right to be King of
the Mountain. But she saw the worry in his eyes when he thought
she was not looking and she knew that sometimes he did doubt.
Right now he was wondering why everything seemed to be
going against him and his family. The man he was now bore little
likeness to that proud boy who had played "King of the

Mountain" in the schoolyard and slagheaps of that time so long ago.

When the courts had still not made a decision on the election results, the Republican school board was told to prepare for the coming school term as if they were the elected governing body. In July 1934, the board met to prepare for the 1934-35 school year. They set September tenth as the date for school opening, and selected teachers and principals. The new principal of the Bruno School was Fred Bruno. On August 30, 1934, the staff went to the school and began enrolling the children. They returned the following day to continue the enrollment process, only to be confronted with a mob of three hundred angry people armed with blackjacks, pick handles, baseball bats and clubs, rocks, chunks of coal and other missiles led by the defeated Democratic candidates. The mob threatened the staff and tried to prevent them from entering the school.

Fred Bruno, the principal, succeeded in getting in, but some of the crowd followed him and demanded that he turn over the keys, while others accosted the teachers. Five days later that same group largely made up of Democratic Party members took possession of the school, installed their own teachers and principal not elected by the school board, and opened the school for attendance. Other mobs attacked the remaining school buildings in similar ways, throwing coal, nailing the doors shut, and taunting the teachers. The Democrat-led groups kept control of the schools until the legally elected school board members filed suit against the usurpers.

At the hearing before the Supreme Court of Pennsylvania, the defendants demanded that the court settle the question of the school board election, but the judge told them that was not the purpose of the hearing. In addition, the defendants were told that they could neither take the law into their own hands, nor "by force and intimidation obtain control of the school buildings or exclude the regularly appointed teachers."

The ruling further stated "no one supposes that either one of the two opposing factions in this community is completely free of blame for creating the present situation. But whatever may be the background of ill will existing between these groups, it does not justify in the slightest the acts of mob violence which are indicated by this record. Such conduct will not be tolerated so long as the regularly constituted courts are in existence."

The Brunos were relieved at the ruling of the court, but it seemed to make little difference to the opposing camp. They continued to hold their open-air meetings, to taunt any and all members of the Bruno family, to threaten the men and harass the women regardless of their age or relationship to Joseph. Few parents were willing to subject their children to possible danger and actual harassment, so the schools remained effectively closed, in spite of the high court's ruling.

"Papa, what are you doing?" Fred asked when he saw Joseph take the new rifle from the staircase hiding place.

"We are in danger."

"We are not!"

"We are in danger and I am going to do everything I can to protect my family!"

"But more guns won't make things safer! If we stay in our homes and don't provoke them ...."

"Why must we be prisoners in our own home, in our own town? I must be able to defend myself and my family!"

Jimmy watched silently from the doorway, his usual look of bland complacency gone, replaced for a moment by a look of fear and confusion. Maybe he should have been more involved with the business, he thought. No, none of this should be his fault. He simply stayed and helped when he had to.

"I'm glad that Ernie's off in school at Hershey and isn't having to suffer through all this," Antoinette had just finished reading her father a letter from her youngest brother. Joseph recalled the time when Antoinette had been away at Kutztown College getting her teaching degree. She had thoroughly enjoyed school and had had few problems even though at that time young girls rarely went away to college.

"Does he like it there, do you think?" Joseph asked, remembering a conversation he had overheard between his parents. He wondered if Ernie had the problems that Joseph's mother, so many years before, had feared he might face at a private school.

"Yes, I think so. He does well, anyway."

As he looked at his daughter, who always stood tall and had a proud stature, much like him at her age, he was amazed at how strong-willed and determined she was for a young woman. He knew he could always count on his little Nettie. He thought, too, about Jimmy; how he was so different from Nettie, and wondered again what had happened to turn him away.

The Republicans met quietly, as they usually did once or twice a week through the autumn of 1934. The schools were still closed and tensions in the county were at a boiling point. After one meeting late in October, Joseph headed back to the house with Fred and Phil.

"Papa, they're out there again—listen to them shouting," Fred said. "I hope they don't come down here again."

"I heard some of them talking about how well they're going to do in November, and how they were going to show the Brunos," Phil said.

"Why are they doing this to us? They act like the whole depression is our fault! They forget how much our family has done for this town and most of the people in it!" Joseph shook his clenched fist in the air.

"Shhh, Papa, keep still. We don't want to start a fight," Fred took his father's arm and tried to steer him into the house.

"Start a fight! What about what they're doing? Those turncoat Republicans! How can the Democrats trust them?"

"Joe, let's go on into the house where we'll have some privacy."

A few men had stopped on the sidewalk, listening to Joseph's words.

"I'm not saying anything wrong," he continued, "nothing that the whole town can't hear. I have rights here, just like everyone else! I have not done anything wrong, nothing that most of the men in this town wouldn't do themselves!"

Joseph realized that in his anger he was speaking a mixture of Italian and English.

"Mr. Bruno, sir, I heard someone say they're going to march past your house," said one of the party members coming out of the hall behind him.

"If they come near my house, so help me God, I'll do what I have to in order to protect my family and my home! It will be self-defense, pure self-defense! No one would question that. If they come past my house and start to attack—No! It would be so foolish if they did! I could pick them off one by one!"

The men standing on the sidewalk stared at Joseph for a moment then turned and quickly walked off toward where the Democrats were gathered. Fred shook his head and he and Phil looked at each other as they led Joseph into the house

CHAPTER 9

THE "PARADE"

Around seven o'clock in the evening of November 5, 1934, the meeting of the Republican party of Kline Township was called to order. The Republican Party headquarters was located, as it had been for years, in the pool hall next to Joseph's home. The back door of the hall opened right into his backyard and its front door was only steps from his house.

The meeting started a few minutes late in the smoke-filled room and appeared to be an ordinary enough beginning for what would become an unbelievable night. The main purpose of the meeting was to review plans for the next day's election and poll coverage. Frank Bruno opened the meeting with an enthusiastic pre-election speech. He spoke of the importance of the election and the necessity of getting everyone to the polls. He then called for the minutes and turned the podium over to Joseph. Joseph, too, gave a brief election-eve pep talk. Everyone was excited about the next day's election. It had been a long campaign and already a bitter contest. All were anxious to see it finally come to a conclusion. Everyone knew that the results of the county and statewide elections could have tremendous consequences on their local matters. If the Republicans won and retained control, it would foretell a victory once and for all as well as the end of the school board fiasco.

All in all, the meeting was uneventful and since everyone needed to get home to prepare for the following day, they quickly adjourned. Several people stayed to talk to Joseph about personal matters and election topics, such as the bus driver who needed to know what to do with the school bus in the morning as it was his duty to take elderly villagers to the polls. Some of the women who would be helping were waiting at Joseph's house for him to sign their poll passes. The passes would allow access to the voting polls so the bearer could monitor the election.

The Democratic meeting, however, was a different story. The assembly had begun at the home of one of the Democratic leaders at the east edge of town. When too many people arrived to fit on the front porch, the group spilled into the yard, then onto the street. About 400 people had gathered and excitement was running high, until, around nine o'clock, the atmosphere became frenzied.

The people were excited and anxious about the election the following day. They believed they had a strong chance of winning at least some of the open offices and felt strongly that it was about time. They hoped that school board issues would be decided in their favor also. A few men spoke, and supporters began to shout some of the party's slogans. Someone cried, "Let's sing the national anthem!"

At this point the crowd was a jumble of men, women, and children. Someone drove up in a large flatbed truck and some of the group began to climb aboard, chanting and waving their arms and fists. They started innocently enough, shouting phrases such as, "Democratic ticket all the way!" "We want change!" and "Vote Democrat!" but then the name of their Republican enemy crept in and the shouts turned to taunts: "Down with the Brunos!" "No more Joe!" "Joe must go."

Unobserved by the crowd, a car pulled to the side of the street about a block north of the gathering. Inside the car, watching the activity, were two young women. No one on the street recognized the car or the women inside—no one even looked at them. If anyone had, he would have seen Antoinette Bruno Billig and her cousin peering through the car windows, their ears picking up the noise of a fanatical mob. The women were listening for hints of what might happen next. They could tell that the horde was in a state of frenzy and would soon be reaching the boiling point. Moments later the crowd spilled into the street, growing louder and larger. Suddenly, someone shouted, "Let's march to Bruno's house! Show them we are not afraid, that we're strong and they can't keep us from voting tomorrow!"

An older man ran from the crowd and yelled, "Wait! Wait for me! I'll be right back!" Clearly he was a leader by the way the people waited, watching as he slipped through the crowd and into his nearby home, emerging with an American flag. As he came to the front of the crowd, he raised the flag above the gathering mob, shouting, "Let's march! Follow me, people! We'll show the Republicans we mean business!"

Three or four men moved randomly through the crowd playing a march with drums and several other instruments. The group tried to organize itself loosely into a line with the flag at the lead, marchers next, and a flatbed truckload of yelling children bringing up the rear. At best it was a ragtag band of people bound by a common cause—a flag and a crowd of loosely gathered marchers do not a parade make.

The group started to march along the side of Center Street. But as more people joined and the rumble of voices grew louder, the crowd filled the street, projecting a more powerful presence. Some tried to organize the crowd as it proceeded. Others joined just to see what was happening and were swept into the chaos. Nearly eight hundred people were now involved, yelling and chanting willy-nilly, and flowing along the street in one direction, toward Fourth and Center Streets and the Bruno home.

Antoinette could hear them approaching as she parked the car in the alley behind her father's home. She and her cousin dashed in to tell the others of the mob that was barely a few blocks away.

The Republican meeting had ended, and her father had returned to the house. He was in his office with Fred and Phil's son Arthur. As usual people were standing in line or sitting on chairs in the hall outside Joe's office door. They looked up as Antoinette ran down the hall. Everyone could tell that something was wrong. They stood up or leaned forward to hear her news, but the door slammed shut behind her as she rushed into her father's office.

"Father! They're headed this way—the Democrats! Four blocks or more down the road heading this direction! What are we going to do? They have sticks and lumps of coal! There are so many of them! They're wild, I tell you—wild! They've been whipped into a frenzy! I'm afraid they're out of control!"

"Hush, dear, hush," Joseph spoke softly, putting his arm around his distraught daughter. "Don't worry, we'll take care of it."

Her father went to the door and said to those waiting, "Leave at once. Go to your homes, your families. It is not a night to be out." Most of the people left the house through the front door, where they could hear the approaching mob as they ran to their homes.

One woman said, "I pray for Joseph and his family. This is not a good night. Only something bad can come of such a crowd!" Then, she, too, ran for home.

Unfortunately, the three women waiting for their poll passes were in one of the parlors downstairs and did not hear Joseph's instructions to leave.

Joseph went downstairs with Antoinette to the kitchen where his wife sat chatting with some other family members. He said to his younger daughter, "Elveda, come with me to the phone. Hurry, we must call the police, now."

Joseph touched his wife's shoulder and said, "Cecilia, take the others and go to the basement! Quickly! Antoinette, help your mother quiet the little ones!"

The women looked at one another in alarm, panic in their eyes, wondering what was wrong. Cecilia and Elinor were hysterically crying and needed reassuring. They gathered up the two little girls huddled on the floor and headed for the basement doorway.

"Uncle Paul!" One of the little girls wriggled out of her grandmother's arms, running off to look for her uncle. Paul did not have time to stop and let her run into his big, strong, outstretched arms and give her a hug, as he usually did. Instead he ran out the side door, to the house across the street, where his father, Phil, was alone and cut off from the rest of the family by the mob running down the street like a river gone wild, overrunning its banks.

Grandmother Cecilia dashed after her, catching her in the hall. Antoinette seeing her mama and two innocent daughters still wandering aimlessly through the house, grabbed her mother's arm and led all three of them to the basement at the back of the house, the farthest point from the angry crowd. She then kissed her girls on the forehead as if she were just putting them to bed on a normal evening, and said softly, "Stay and help your grandma until I get back."

Antoinette ran upstairs, two flights, and saw Elveda dialing the phone. She was out of breath and could not say another word without panting and gasping for air. Joseph turned to Antoinette with a deep hollow glare as if in another world. Elveda dialed and asked the operator for the State Police. The phone line started to ring and as soon as she heard a voice on the other end, she handed the receiver to her father.

He spoke quietly, but firmly, "This is Joseph Bruno of Kelayres. Please send troopers right away to my home. An angry, disorderly mob is descending upon us. Send help now! Please hurry!"

"I'm sorry sir, but you have been connected to the Hazelton Barracks, not the Tamaqua Barracks. The Tamaqua Barracks would be in the jurisdiction of your home in Kelayres. You will have to call them."

Joseph hung up the telephone and told Elveda what had happened, asking her to try again. This time the operator connected them to the trooper station in Tamaqua. Joseph repeated his request, more urgently this time, as the front of the mob was actually approaching the nearby street corner.

When Joseph was told they were being dispatched, he hung up the telephone and told his two daughters to go downstairs to their mother. Nothing was left for them to do. He turned to the nearest window where he could see people coming in the direction of the church and his home.

As the crowd moved closer to the Bruno home, the people became even more disorganized, like the loose tentacles of an octopus flowing in several directions at once, yet knotted together at the center. As they rounded the corner of Fourth and Center Streets some turned to the right, others to the left. Those going to the left were headed away, farther down the street from the house, but when they saw the other arm of the mob turn toward the house, they paused uncertainly. They had not intended to confront the Bruno's by passing the house on two sides. It was getting late. They had had their fun, made their point and were ready to go home, but the other arm of the group continued until it stopped right in front of the house.

Joseph ran down the stairs and flung open the side kitchen door, shouting, "Go home! Go back where you came from! No good can come from this!"

The mob booed him loudly and he slammed the door shut. He paused a second to take a breath, then ran through the kitchen to the back hall and to the top of the basement stairs, to check on his wife, daughters and granddaughters, frightened and huddled at the bottom of the staircase. From there he hurried back upstairs, straight to the window where Fred stood looking out. As Joseph arrived, something hit the streetlight at the corner which exploded into shattering flakes of glass. People started screaming. Joseph yelled toward the stairway, "It's all right—just stay down! I think someone's shooting!"

With the light out he could barely see the people approaching the corner at Fourth and Center by the church. Then he heard a loud crack! And something hit the frame of the window. Joseph and Fred dropped to the floor. As he peered over the window-sill, Joseph heard shouts and screams of panic from both outside and inside the house. Joseph and Fred looked at each other then carefully got to their feet.

As the crowd began to approach Jimmy's house on Center Street, next door on the far side of the family lot, Jimmy was walking across the yard, just about to enter his father's back door. He heard a sharp sound ring out in the night air, followed by the shattering of glass, and the night sky got even darker. Jimmy dropped to his knees and half ran, half crawled to the back door just as his father ran downstairs to the front door.

The sound had been a gunshot blowing out the corner street light, sending shards of broken glass into those at the front of the crowd. A few women screamed, children ran in every direction, and some froze where they stood. To the crowd closest to the street light the sound was thought to be gunshots. Those farther back thought it was just a firecracker, or maybe a shot into the air intended to disperse the crowd. No one realized what was about to happen.

Now that his eyes had adjusted to the dark, Joseph could see more clearly that people were running in every direction. He heard Jimmy call as he ran into the house from the backyard, "Papa, where are you? Are you all right?"

As he entered the back hall, Jimmy heard his mother call his name. He looked down the basement stairs and saw his mother and the other women huddled together at the bottom of the cellar steps, crying and shaking.

"Don't worry, Mama! It will be all right! Go into the root cellar and bolt the door."

Jimmy knew why the crowd was there—they wanted his father, not the women. After all it was his father who was the center of power and who had offered the most resistance to their political plans.

"Go take care of your father, James, my darling, be careful," Cecilia called to him from down the stairs.

"Yes, Mama! Stay down there and bolt the door no matter what happens," warned Jimmy.

It was suddenly clear to Jimmy what was important—his family. This was no time to dwell on what had happened in the past. His family was in danger and he had to help.

Joseph and Fred had assembled the family's collection of guns and ammunition from their various storage places throughout the house. Fred was trying to sort them on the bed in Joseph and Cecilia's room, matching guns with ammunition. He and Joseph each picked up a gun and some ammunition and began to load. Fred finished and rushed off to the adjacent room while Joseph stood by his bureau, trying to load bullets into the rifle he had bought only days before. He had spent several leisurely hours on the mountainside with Phil learning how to load and handle it, but now, with an angry mob roaring just outside his home and his family in danger, he was having great difficulty. He stopped and laid down the weapon, wiping beads of perspiration from his forehead, then held his two hands tightly together to stop the shaking. He thought of Cecilia and his daughters and the other women hiding in the basement, of those people outside who were threatening his family and his home, and suddenly a great calm filled him.

Silence filled his ears and his mind grew quiet. He picked up the weapon and carefully loaded it, this time with ease, then turned to the window. In the few seconds before he opened it, he looked out into the night, at the mob outside, waving their arms, flinging stones and hunks of coal toward the house, and it was as if he were watching a silent movie. Suddenly there was a crash as a rock flew through the window next to him, sending glass flying everywhere. He threw up the sash in front of him and knelt down, glass crunching under his feet, and raised the gun's sight to his eye.

Cecilia was calm, too, as calm as she had ever felt in her life. So long had this time been coming, the tension building, the moment of truth brewing, it was almost a relief now that it was here. Now it was all up to God and the state troopers for they would be here any minute and see once and for all the troublemakers attacking the family's home. She held her granddaughters close as they sat huddled on the bottom step in the darkened basement. They could see the dim shapes of the small windows at ground level, but they faced the back of the house, not the street.

"How many were there?" she whispered to Antoinette.

"I don't know—hundreds! They were wild, Mama! Oh, God, please help us! Help Papa!"

"Yes, my dear, that's what we do now, we pray. God help us!"

They heard the back door slam and the face of Cecilia's nephew Tony appeared at the top of the stairs.

"Go to your uncle, Tony!"

"Yes, Auntie!"

Then stillness, some shouts, and a very loud crack. Elveda, her younger daughter, screamed. Her two granddaughters were shaking but silent as if in shock.

"Hush, dear! It's all right. We must be calm."

"Mama, I'm so frightened!" Elveda pleaded, clutching her mother's waist. Her hold was so tight she almost ripped apart the apron her mother still wore.

"Yes, dear, I know. Pray to Mary. Think of her smiling face in the church, the church right across the street. Think of being back in church with the sun shining."

Then they heard more footsteps upstairs and Phil's voice calling down to them. He was out of breath as he had just run in from his house across the street.

"Cecilia? You all right?"

"We're all right, Uncle Phil—go help Papa!" Antoinette shouted.

"I'm going!" Phil shouted back.

The women heard another crack, then another, and more, coming close together now. Cecilia thought of the long package she saw Joseph carry into the house the week before when he thought she was not there.

"Oh, Dearest Jesus, protect them!"

The women could hear the men throughout the house calling back and forth to one another, asking if they were all right and what was happening at their vantage point. When they heard their voices they were reassured that everyone was still alright.

Meanwhile, next door at Jimmy's house, a large coal chunk went sailing through the front window. The family housekeeper, who was in her eighties, was almost hit by the missile and the shattering glass.

"Papa!" shouted Jimmy, peering up the darkened stairway at his father's house. "Where are you?

"Up here, Jimmy! Stay low! Get up here as fast as you can!" his father shouted back."

Jimmy ran to the bedroom to where the guns and ammunition were dumped on the bed. Joseph was at the window shooting into the air and yelling, "Stop, I say! Stop this nonsense! Go home!"

Jimmy picked up a weapon and ran to the bedroom on the side of the house where his brother Fred was already stationed at the window. He knelt beside Fred. In the next room their father was doing the same, guarding their home and family. More shots came from across the street and several windows broke as chunks of coal sailed through the night sky. It seemed by the small bursts of red flashes that the shots were coming from across the street near Saladago's.

Time stopped for Joseph. There was only the crowd outside, threatening his family and his home, and the gun in his hands. There was no past, no future—there was only now, only his beloved wife in the basement, weeping quietly and praying; his children—his devoted daughters, his brave sons nearby, his trusted brother Phil and his nephews moving from room to room, offering what help they could. Across the street he could see his nephews Anthony and Arthur moving from room to room in his brother's house.

Joseph then heard the sounds of a woman nearby crying nervously. He called out "Who's there?" It turned out to be one of the three women who had been waiting in an adjoining room for their poll passes. They had run and hidden between two beds when the others had left the house. Now they were frightened and caught between the lines of gunfire. Joseph called to them to get under the beds and stay still. The women looked at each other in shock and rolled under the nearby beds.

The scene outside was like a thunderstorm, with brilliant flashes of light breaking through a sky made darker by contrast, thunderous roars shaking the ground, the windows and panicked screams splintering the night. Then, in only a few minutes, a few minutes that had felt like a lifetime, it was over. The guns and the screams were quiet.

The crowd had escaped into the darkness of the shadowy streets. Some had run to the church, others to the drug store around the corner. More than a few children hid under the church steps. Some people crouched behind shrubs or a mailbox, or in the front yards of nearby homes. A few lay in the street, not moving.

There was a time of eerie silence, then a low murmur began to rise as people slipped out to help those lying in the street. When it was clear that no more shots would be fired more and more people came out of hiding, some carrying the injured to houses or to cars.

Fearing the worst, two details of state troopers were on the way to the scene, coming from both directions, as the Tamaqua squadron leader had radioed the Hazelton barracks for reinforcements,. If the crowd was as large and wild as reports claimed the troopers knew they would need all the help they could get, regardless of jurisdiction.

But by the time law enforcement arrived, there were no parading crowds, no yelling mob, no riot and no further need of force. The scene that confronted the troopers was one of chilling agony. The troopers had arrived too late to stop the political confrontation that had been brewing for months.

People were lying in the street in pools of their own blood; others crying or yelling for help. Some people had already crawled to safety; some were being carried to cars headed for Hazelton Hospital. It was deep into the night, and though there was usually some light in the town from streetlights, now there was simply an eerie darkness, broken only by headlights and lanterns.

Within minutes of seeing the troopers arrive, a smaller crowd began reforming outside the Bruno home, starting to grow loud and threatening again. The mob appeared to be coming back to life although it was much smaller.

The troopers made their way through the throng of angry people and stood along the brick wall that Joseph's father James had built so many years before. Some of the troopers even stood on the brick wall. Their uniformed and armed presence helped calm the situation.

The commanding officer and several more troopers entered the gate to the Bruno home. They went to the side door and Joseph himself opened the door for the commander. They all entered the kitchen, where they could see some of the women of the family emerging from the cellar. They could hear the crowd shouting, "Get the Brunos! Hang Joe Bruno! He's a murderer!"

Cecilia ran to Joseph's side and clung to him as he stood calmly, silently, but always straight and proud, watching the members of various law enforcement services pour into his home. More troopers arrived to investigate and protect the family against the mob outside. Rumors were circulating that they had dynamite stolen from the mines and were going to blow up the large brick family home.

The scene at the Hazleton Hospital was one of horror and confusion. The nurses were receiving wounded patients coming in private cars and eventually in ambulances and state trooper vehicles. Three men were confirmed dead upon arrival. Others were in critical condition needing immediate attention, sometimes right in the hallway as they arrived. One of those men died the next morning of his wounds and another several days later.

Five dead men in all, and twenty or so injured, some gravely, others less so. Most of the injured had several wounds as if sprayed by BB guns. Many loved ones wounded or dead. Countless families destroyed. All because of an election.

The state police searched the upstairs of Joseph's house and found three women still huddled under two beds, and a fourth crouched behind a sofa downstairs. All were shaken and almost hysterical, but despite their condition the police interrogated them on the spot. They made statements they would not even remember.

Officers outside tried to quiet the crowd and disperse them, or at least keep them across the street from the house. Reinforcements were sent in from Reading to allow for a human chain of protection around the entire estate, which took up almost an entire block.

Troopers also entered Phil's house across the street and Jimmy's home behind Joseph's. Jimmy's elderly housekeeper and his wife were brought to the main house, as were Phil, his son Paul, and both their wives. After hours of searching and investigation, the troopers drove the fourteen collected family members and guests to the Tamaqua barracks for further questioning. Though it was now the early hours of the morning, everyone was anxious to prove his or her version of the story. Some troopers remained behind at the family home to guard against looting and vandalism.

That night when troopers searched the upstairs rooms, they found weapons and ammunition throughout. The next day, troopers found additional guns and ammunition upstairs, although some of the armaments, not seen earlier, seemed to have appeared overnight while the family members were at the state trooper station in Tamaqua. The police, after hearing reports that "numerous secret compartments" were in the home, did not feel they had found everything, so they asked the builder of the house for a floor plan. Because of the shape of the roof, storage areas were located in all four corners of the second floor accessible only through closets. But when the officers searched them, they found, instead of machine guns, the family's winter clothes and some dusty, unused furniture.

In the staircase, four or five steps from the first floor landing, they discovered a loose step which proved to be a trapdoor that opened upward on hinges. Inside they found some ammunition that was still unopened, but apparently most of that stash had been grabbed when the shooting started.

Both upstairs and in the kitchen they found stones and chunks of coal mixed with shards of glass. Several windows had been broken and bullet holes riddled the bedroom and kitchen walls. Jimmy's house also had several broken windows and a large rock on the stairway, which the housekeeper would later testify was thrown by a member of the mob. The street lights had apparently been broken by someone who wanted to make it more difficult to see what was going on.

The next day when Joseph's wife and daughters returned home from being questioned, the house was in a shambles. The mob had broken more windows and police had overturned many pieces of furniture in their investigation. Fragile items had been smashed and more than a few expensive pieces were missing. Among the missing pieces were jewelry and a watch which Joseph's father had brought from Italy years earlier. While the family was gone that first night hundreds of dollars disappeared from the safe. The money was never recovered, nor were the vanished family heirlooms. Cecilia's mother's family portrait was ripped, as if someone had broken the glass and then used a shard to tear the canvas, to see if anything were hidden behind it. They had found nothing but threw the remains on the floor anyway. Cecilia later crouched down to pick up the pieces, holding the torn shreds together as though trying to restore her family to what it had been only hours earlier.

The physical state of the home was not the only damage done. The family was nearly destroyed; seven of its members were still in jail awaiting arraignment. The women were allowed to enter the home for necessities, but it was more than a week before they were allowed to return to stay. Even then they had to live in the home with police quartered upstairs, as well as across the street in the church basement, which had become a virtual police station.

The family was living with daily threats and bomb scares; they were assaulted and harassed if they went outside. In spite of the fact that the family was concealed behind the drawn curtains and recently boarded windows they could not help noticing the reporters and onlookers outside the house at all hours, pointing and whispering.

News of the election eve gunfight had spread rapidly throughout the eastern United States. Headlines took on the fervor of a campaign to smear Republicans on a national scale. "The Kelayres Massacre" was emblazoned in the *New York Times, Philadelphia Inquirer,* and the *Chicago Tribune.* "Many dead or injured as Republican party leader opens fire on Democratic election eve 'parade' in a small coal mining town," read one story line. Reporters came to the tiny village from across the Eastern Seaboard. The survivors subsided into two camps. Neither side could discern the truth any longer. The stakes were too high.

The election of 1934 was seen as a test for the New Deal Democrats. The Democratic national chairman said, "The Roosevelt tide is running full steam ahead in this country and will not be denied." Both parties had had high expectations on the eve of that election.

Thirty-three state governorships were up for election across the country, as well as many Senate seats. Seven states were also voting on prohibition. Much was at stake in that election year. The Pennsylvania Democrats wanted to wrest the reins of power from the Republican Party, which had occupied the Governor's mansion since the Civil War.

After news of the Kelayres massacre had spread, William A. Schnader, the state's Republican gubernatorial candidate and state's attorney general at the time, issued a statement, declaring, "Disorder arising from partisan or factional excitement is always deplored and doubly so when attended by loss of life." He then promised his full support for an investigation to bring about the prosecution of those responsible. He indicated he would not hesitate to assign a special prosecutor to lead the investigation.

At his final campaign rally, Attorney General Schnader cried out, "Better times are coming! If we vote sensibly, we'll have better times much faster. I know the people of Pennsylvania, and I know their answer to this sort of mudslinging campaign. The answer will be a complete victory everywhere for the Republican Party!"

An editorial in the morning edition of the *Philadelphia Inquirer* on Election Day stated, "The eyes of the nation are on Pennsylvania, which is unshaken by the winds of political sophistry, and stands like a rock for the principles and ideals of stable representative government."

The people of the town of Kelayres, though submerged in grief, turned out for the election, voting the Democrats into office in a landslide victory. The tallied ballots came in 634–24 favoring the Democrats. Such were unheard of results for the area. Fear endangered by the previous night's bloodshed kept many away from the polls, especially on the Republican side of the ballot. The Democrats, with nothing to fear and with their rivals in jail, turned out in droves.

A few days later, on November 9, 1934, huge crowds from all over the country filled the streets to honor the five dead men. Elected officials from all over the state were present for the funeral events, including the new governor and senator-elect. All the funerals were held in McAdoo and Kelayres with two of them being held at the Immaculate Conception Italian Church across the street from the Bruno family compound.

The funeral procession started on Main Street in McAdoo, passing the bank, saloon, and other of the Bruno properties. The hearses, draped in black and five abreast, worked their way slowly down the streets that were lined with people. The post office, the schools, the collieries, and all the businesses were closed. The Screen Gems newsreel of the event captured it all for the national audience, with a special showing that weekend in the Palace Theater in McAdoo. Reporters from as far away as Chicago were rushed to the area to report on the election eve massacre and funerals. It was a huge story of the election process gone wrong.

But was the truth being told?

After the funerals, the local constabulary gave the visiting dignitaries a tour of the Bruno home, as if it were a local carnival attraction. When some of the grieving widows were visited personally by the dignitaries, they begged for revenge. Ironically, several of these women who were yelling their pleas and insults in Italian, were some of the very people the Brunos had brought over for jobs and a better life. It was a horrible day made even worse by all the reporters trying to stir up more hysteria and anger.

The Bruno family could not have participated, whether they may have wanted to or not. They had become outcasts in their own town, the town they had helped to build, and now they were prisoners in their own homes.

After they were allowed to return to their home, Cecilia and her daughters gathered the remaining family members together as often as they could. But even so, they had no privacy, as the police and FBI were constantly in and out of the house pursuing their investigations.

The press had a field day with the tragedy, delighted to have something exciting to report on, something other than the depression. One early interview quoted Joseph as insisting, "I haven't done anything. Everybody's story has been told but mine."

The reporter wrote, "Lodged in a small cell with his son Alfred, the 50-year-old county detective who came to this country at the age of 18 months and who made himself a small political kingdom in Kline Township, was nervously puffing a cigar throughout the day."

"There isn't anything strange about the guns being found in my house," the paper goes on to quote Joseph as saying. "My family likes hunting. One gun was my father's, another mine, still another, my brother-in-law's. The revolvers? Well, I used one in my detective work. A few were given to me as gifts by friends."

Several days later when Antoinette dared to look back, it was all a blur. And that was just fine with her—it was too awful to think about. Why did it happen? Times were hard and everyone was working hard for so little, but it had not needed to come to this.

Antoinette stood looking out the window over Center Street, empty now except for ghosts and echoes of the mob, the shots, the screams, of that awful night. Everything was different now. Her life and her family's lives, the lives of everyone in the town had been changed, suddenly and irrevocably.

She turned and sat down wearily in the old rocking chair, one her grandfather had bought so her grandmother could rock the little ones to sleep; one that had been in the family for so many years. She leaned back and closed her eyes, breathing a long sad sigh. A tear slipped from each eye and rolled down her smooth cheeks.

I need to get up and see about Mama, Antoinette thought, sitting up and opening her eyes. Quickly wiping away her tears, she squared her shoulders, took a deep breath and held her head high in the way she'd been taught, the way that was in her blood, her body—the Bruno way they called it, proud as a peacock.

But just as she was about to stand, she caught sight of the photo of that young family, the first ones to come to Kelayres, or Bunker Hill, as it was called back then. The photograph's glass was shattered, its frame askew from the violence it had suffered that tragic night. She picked it up and sank back in the rocker, remembering stories her grandmother Marie Antonia had told her, rocking her in this very chair. She had told her stories of the old country and of the gradual fulfillment of the family's dream as it unfolded in the beautiful mountains of Pennsylvania which echoed for the family members the mountains of their beloved Calabria.

CHAPTER 10

THE TRIALS

The arraignment of the Bruno family members was highly controversial. Both sides presented arguments on behalf of their clients. The Bruno family lawyers tried unsuccessfully to have all charges dropped on the premise that the family members were returning gunfire after their homes had been surrounded and attacked by an angry mob. But seven members of the Bruno family were indicted on thirty-five counts anyway. Those indicted were Joseph Bruno and his sons Alfred and James, Joseph's brother Phil, two of Phil's sons, Paul and Arthur, and another nephew, Tony.

The first trial began Monday, January 7, 1935: The trial, a major event in the county, was well attended by both sides. Extra chairs were moved into the county courtroom, and vouchers for admittance were handed out to people on the steps of the courthouse. Many were not admitted inside and remained in the halls and on the steps of the courthouse in the frigid cold of the mountain winter. Joseph Bruno was charged with the murder of the first victim to fall dead on that fateful night, Frank Fiorilla.

At first, Joseph, his family and their attorneys were confident, certain that their argument of self-defense would succeed, that the trial was merely a formality. Though the men of the family were not in attendance—they had been denied release on bail—Joseph's wife and daughters were, and throughout the trial and court proceedings Joseph spoke freely to them as they sat behind him. He often smiled at friends and neighbors who testified and glared at those that swore under oath against him.

The press watched Joseph's every move and reported each like tattle-tale schoolchildren: "He arrived at the courthouse dressed in a tailor-made gray suit and an imported dark fedora." "On many occasions he takes off his tortoise-shell framed spectacles and wipes his forehead with a freshly pressed silk handkerchief." "He is constantly using his pocket knife to clean or trim his finger nails." "He moved his head so he could not see the face of a victim's wife as she testified."

During recesses and breaks, acquaintances or political supporters would speak to Joseph—sometimes the chats were friendly, other times, business discussions. Joseph would give advice on matters or hand out orders for tasks that needed to be performed. Teachers from the schools would also seek him out.

Throughout their entire stay at the county facility Joseph's son, Alfred, continued in office as president of the school board. He continued to sign pay checks and help control the budget and handle daily school affairs from either the courtroom or the jail. The entire time the Bruno family were prisoners in the county jail, they were never handcuffed or even touched by the guards. They were merely asked to return to the jail with the guards. The prisoners were also allowed to talk privately with family members and friends in the courtroom.

At first, newspapers across the country, including the *New York Times* and *Chicago Tribune*, carried the story on their front pages as headline news. But soon business-as-usual returned and other events pushed news of the Bruno trial to inside pages. In an ironic twist of fate, Bruno Hauptmann was also being tried at the same time for the kidnapping and murder of the baby of Charles Lindbergh. Newspaper headlines echoed one another as the words "Bruno" and "trial" repeatedly appeared in duplicate. One overzealous reporter even tried to link the two events just because the name "Bruno" was involved in both events.

On January 15, 1935, the courtroom was not as crowded as many people, mostly Democrats, had traveled to Harrisburg for the state inauguration festivities, the proceeds of which were earmarked for aid to the families of the Kelayres massacre victims.

January 21 saw the orderly reopening of the Kline Township schools. More than four hundred children were present, most escorted by their mothers. Twelve teachers were in attendance, some of whom had to leave early to testify.

Joseph's defense team was led by his nephew Frank Bruno, who had been admitted to the bar barely a year earlier. Many witnesses testified in Joseph's favor. Some witnesses were political friends and supporters, others were family members, and still others were people who lived in the town or were church members.

Some witnesses placed Joe inside Republican headquarters at the time four young men said he was outside and they heard him say he "would knock them off one by one." Had that statement been true, it would have established premeditation, an intent to murder in cold blood.

Others swore that they had seen or heard shots fired from outside the home and that the men on the other side of the street had fired first. They had shot their own friends and their own families. In addition, they claimed they had seen men with guns and flashes of gunfire from the porch next to the post office. It was introduced that unfortunately a family feud existed within the Democratic leadership and some of the local leaders were not pleased with one another. So the testimonies ended up being simply confusing. In the end not enough evidence could be found to prove that theory.

One of the witnesses from the prosecution side, when questioned as to his own involvement in the murders and shootings, simply shouted, "My name is not Joe Bruno!" The crowd, lulled close to sleep in the heat and closeness of the old courtroom, awoke with a roar at the statement. The judge banged his gavel, over and over, as people jumped to their feet. Reporters shouted; flashbulbs popped.

"Order, I say! Order in the court!"

Another rousing episode in the trials occurred when the elderly housekeeper of the Bruno family testified that the mob had thrown rocks through the windows of Jimmy's house where she had been at the time. She said she feared for her life and was afraid that the mob would enter the house or set it on fire. She went on to say, "If I had had a gun, I would have shot back!"

The Bruno family members and their defense team could barely contain their reactions. Meanwhile, everyone in the courtroom laughed out loud at the thought of an elderly woman in her eighties brandishing a shotgun.

Defense witnesses spoke highly of the good deeds and reputation of the Bruno family. Still others testified of the angry mob that marched through the town and surrounded the Bruno home. Some said they overheard that the mob had dynamite; others heard chants of "Get the Brunos!" Witnesses said windows in the Bruno home had been broken with stones and chunks of coal thrown by the mob. Others testified everyone in the mob carried a club or chunks of coal— even the children.

More than one witness claimed to have seen a mysterious man in an expensive overcoat and fedora shoot out the street light, the act that had started the worst of the chaos. Allegedly, the man then ran to a waiting yellow car that quickly drove off toward McAdoo. Neither the man nor the yellow car could be located.

The legal team for the Commonwealth of Pennsylvania had many witnesses as well. Some swore they saw Joe Bruno in the window holding a gun. They said they saw bursts of flame again and again coming from the Bruno home. Some said they saw James Bruno in the yard along the hedge hidden by the brick garden wall with a gun. Saw shots. Saw men fall. Saw James run into the house through the back door carrying a gun.

Some of the witnesses even stumbled and fell in the stand, tripping over words, questions, times, distances. They were confused, contradicted themselves and finally broke down. Again and again, the Bruno defense team caught them in their lies and stories that appeared to have been made up from the rumors which abounded everywhere.

One witness testified that she had seen Joseph Bruno at an upstairs window firing on the crowd in the so-called parade. During cross-examination she admitted that she had recently lost her home due to foreclosure by the bank of which Joseph was a director. The defense suggested that she had ill feelings toward the accused, but she replied in broken English, "I no angry!" and her testimony was allowed to stand.

Another witness, one of the women Joseph had heard crying from under the bed during the terror, testified in favor of the state, but under reexamination changed her testimony in favor of Joseph. She was an important witness, as she was actually in the Bruno home during the attack. She testified that Joseph was protecting his family as well as herself and her two companions. In her testimony, she described the house as under siege. When questioned on the night of the massacre, she originally stated that she had seen Joseph fire into the crowd. That piece of forced testimony amid the hysterical moments of the chaos, was not her entire account. She was never questioned that night as to when the shooting started, or who had started firing shots first. Was Joseph shooting before the shots from outside were fired? Was he returning shots or did he fire first? Her testimony was largely omitted because of her alleged change of story.

The first trial ended after many bitter battles between the two teams of attorneys and four long weeks of testimony that seemed to lean first one way, then the other. The jury was left to sort through hours and hours of testimony, of lawyers and the judge admonishing them to think this and believe that, but to decide "beyond a shadow of a doubt—so help you God!" what was the truth. What a difficult task the jury members had before them: to decide a man's fate. And the task took its toll.

One woman juror, on the fourth day of deliberation, was unable to leave her bed in the dormitory that had been set up for the members. So the jurors debated at her bedside, summoning a physician who said if she didn't improve quickly, she would need an emergency appendectomy.

Frank Bruno, the lead attorney on the Bruno side, received a threatening letter the day before the verdict was given, terrorizing his life and family if he was able to get Joseph acquitted. The threat did not faze Frank, for many such threats had been received throughout the trial, some to him, many to the rest of the family, especially the women. The jury members had also received threats, one having delayed a field trip to the crime scene. One threat was even sent to the *Hazleton Tribune*, written in red ink to lend a deeper sense of its blood-chilling intention.

Tensions were still high, and anger was the order of the day. Kelayres was such a small town and so many people were involved on either side that no one was left unchanged by the event. Everyone in town waited for the jury members to decide the outcome. Finally, after nineteen ballots, they were ready.

Nineteen ballots had to be taken to decide the fate of Joseph Bruno. The jurors deadlocked after the first vote. Then they voted eighteen additional times before they could reach a compromise. The foreman of the jury stood before a hushed, half-empty courtroom to deliver the verdict because the jury had given such short notice.

All eyes were on the jury but the onlookers sat ready to shift their gaze back to Joseph who sat, as always, calm and collected. He wore a pressed suit and had his fedora by his side. With his tortoise shell glasses and freshly cut hair, he appeared normal and calm.

"Will you please read the verdict?" the judge instructed.

"Yes, sir. We the members of the jury find the defendant guilty of manslaughter."

Joseph did not flinch, merely sat calmly, as one of his counsels leaned to say a word to him. The jury had reached a verdict so suddenly that Cecilia had been unable to get to the courthouse. So Joseph faced the news alone. Pain gripped her heart as she thought of him, so proud, so strong, holding his head high, acting every inch the part of the confident business and civic leader, but she knew that deep within, he was not so confident, not any more. He was concerned, a bit worried, maybe a little frightened. Cecilia knew her beloved husband well.

Every morning for a few seconds when Cecilia woke, the day seemed bright and new, a gift from God, as her mother used to say. Then she would remember. Four weeks. Though it had seemed to last forever, it was over all too soon and her husband was not only still in jail, but sentenced to stay there much longer. Though the sun might be shining, the sky clear and blue, it was not a bright day at all. It was just another dark day. Five of her neighbors were dead and her husband and sons were in jail—on trial possibly for their own lives.

Joseph Bruno was not really sure what had happened that night months earlier—he had told her so in one of the rare moments they had been alone. That was how she knew of his fear. He had never confided in her before—only to his cousin Louis, then Phil, or Jimmy or Fred, even Antoinette, but never to her, his wife. Joseph understood his duty thoroughly—to protect his woman from all harm. His way of doing that was to keep most of his life hidden from her. Little did he know that Cecilia knew everything about him.

Everyone in town knew about Joe Bruno's life, his business and his connections. He was so smart, so savvy, about many things, but sometimes so blind, so lost in his own old-fashioned world. Like now, all he was thinking about was making sure she had enough money to run the house. Of course there was enough money. But what about her heart, her spirit? What about her life, her day-to-day life? From now on, maybe until the day she died, this pain, this grief, this sorrow, this loneliness would belong to her. Her whole life had been blown apart in only a few minutes on that dark autumn night. What had he been thinking? Of her, of course, of protecting her—but at what price?

"We'll appeal, that's all. We'll appeal!" Joseph, in the privacy of his jail cell, displayed the agitation he never showed in public. Frank nodded while the other counselors, older men, former judges, looked at each other, then nodded, one saying, "Yes, of course, Joe. We'll appeal."

"First, we have the other trials," another of the attorneys said, reminding everyone that there was still a long way to go. Only one person had been tried thus far, and for only one murder. There were still four additional murders to try and six other defendants to represent, all family members,

The second trial did not begin until a motion for a change in venue was heard. The Commonwealth's argument was that the Bruno family had too much influence in the county and therefore could not get a fair trial. As in the first trial, many witnesses had had dealings with the accused, some held grudges from the outcome of these dealings, and still others were political foes. Many of the county officials were close friends of the family and several had worked with Joseph, as he had held county offices himself. The judge ruled that the trial would not be moved to a new venue. Instead, a new judge would be appointed, one from another county, who could be neutral in hearing the case.

The new judge heard arguments as to whether the defendants should all be tried at the same time. On May 6, 1935, the second trial began, with the judge's announcement that the trial would be of Joseph Bruno only, for the murder of three of the other victims of the election eve massacre.

The family attorneys objected strenuously to this format, the time and expense of such a series of individual trials on one charge each would be an impossible challenge and burden. After many weeks arguing their case to the court, they were allowed to present their defense for all of the family members that were being held.

The argument was an important one, as the first trial had been only for Joseph and only for one murder charge. It was thought that it would be in the Bruno's favor to try many cases and defend all the charged family members at one time. The family had the money to defend itself, but the trials were going to exact severe emotional cost as well.

After the change of judges, the second trial began in earnest. Additional witnesses were called and new testimony was added. Because more time had passed, many of the testimonies appeared to change. As the Democrats now had political control and the Brunos were locked up, the support of many people had turned away from them.

The second trial lasted several weeks and by the end of the spring of 1935 went to the jury. This time the jury reached a clear decision. A crowded courtroom listened as the verdict was read. Joseph Bruno was found guilty and sentenced to life in the state prison, Philip was sentenced to ten to twenty years for his involvement, and the younger men were all acquitted of any wrongdoing.

The crowd came to life at the reading of this verdict. Some women yelled, "Murderers!" while others from both sides openly sighed. Many thought it was unfair that the younger men were acquitted, while others felt a life sentence was too severe.

"This is ludicrous, Uncle Joe! How can they think that you, a leader in this town for so many years, would do something so foolish as to kill people, your own neighbors, intentionally? Kill them in cold blood! It doesn't make sense!"

"We know that, Frank, but this new Democratic government doesn't seem to see things that way. They want to make us pay, make me pay, for all they haven't had for all these years."

"If my dad were here, he'd know how to deal with this, he'd get us out of all this," Frank said.

Frank wasn't belittling himself when he said that—he knew there was no comparison between them. His father had so much more experience, but more than that he had confidence, a presence, and he had known about people, could read them, could work with them, talk with them, and he had known the people of the Kline Township legal system best of all.

"If your dad were still here, we wouldn't be in all this trouble," Jimmy said quietly, casting a furtive glance at the jail around them.

Frank looked at Jimmy and for a moment he thought he saw tears in his eyes, but then Jimmy stood up, a smile across his face, and said, "I guess I'd better get back in my cell in case some Democrat comes in."

The situation was especially difficult for Jimmy. He had stayed in the background for many years, barely involving himself in the family business. That night he had acted quickly, making a split-second decision to side with his family who were in great danger. He did not regret that decision. He only thought that perhaps he should have done something sooner. Perhaps if he had involved himself in the family business earlier, he could have somehow acted to avoid everything that happened that terrible night.

The third trial began with the state charging several of the family members and witnesses with perjury. In addition, Antoinette was accused of trying to give a bribe of twenty dollars to a man for providing favorable testimony for the family. Several allegations of bribery on both sides were raised, none of which could be substantiated. After just two days, all of the perjury charges were dropped. There were so many to deal with that both sides decided that pursuing such a course of action would be fruitless.

Following the perjury trial, the Bruno men were then charged with the murder of the fifth victim, the man who had died the following day from his injuries the night of the massacre. The defense argued that the death was not a murder. After another long trial, the jury members went into deliberation yet again. But the deliberations took only a few hours.

"Will you please read the verdict?" hearing the judge's instruction, the crowd was reminded of the previous trials. By this time the people were getting used to the suspense.

"Yes, sir. The verdict is as follows: Joseph Bruno, guilty of murder in the first degree, life in prison."

A shout rose in the courtroom. The judge banged furiously with his gavel; eventually order was restored.

"Philip Bruno, guilty of murder in the first degree, life in prison."

Another clamor of outspoken voices was heard, but it quickly died down as the remainder of the verdicts were read.

"James Bruno, guilty of manslaughter."

"Alfred Bruno, guilty of manslaughter."

"Arthur Bruno, guilty of manslaughter."

"Anthony Orlando, guilty of manslaughter."

"Paul Bruno, not guilty." A sigh of relief from some was heard.

Philip shouted, "Shame! Shame!" pointing at the jury after hearing the verdicts. The judge said, "You sit down and be quiet or you will be in contempt of court!"

The crowd was on its feet, too, shouting, pointing and talking among themselves. Supporters and family members were angered with these verdicts, having expected the younger men to be acquitted again.

The anti-Bruno faction was overjoyed as if they felt that justice had been dealt.

The Bruno attorneys called for an appeal to the State Supreme Court of Pennsylvania. The legal team wrote appeals for all the defendants for verdicts from all three trials. It was a very costly effort, the family had already paid seventy-five thousand dollars for the defense attorneys, and now over a thousand pages were typed and compiled into what proved to be a book supporting the appeal. The appeal itself, with all the additional costs paid to the attorneys, cost more than ten thousand dollars by the time everything was assembled and printed. All the preparation for the appeals took several months followed by a waiting period before the case could be scheduled on the docket of the State Supreme Court of Pennsylvania.

The delay was desirable in the eyes of the attorneys for the family. They wanted to drag the process out until the next election in November of 1936, when they believed the Republican Party would regain control at the state and national levels. This was not to be—the Democratic Party won the presidential election and swept most of the offices in Pennsylvania as well. All hope of a favorable political climate in the State Supreme Court faded, and, as feared, the court denied the appeal on the grounds that there was not enough new evidence.

The decision devastated the family. The trials they thought were going to be formalities had gone drastically wrong. All hope for a favorable court-mandated outcome, for redemption of the Bruno name and honor was also gone. The family had been irreparably damaged by the courts' actions. The costs were staggering, and their loved ones were still incarcerated and looking at long sentences.

Now that the appeal was lost, the men were in danger of being transferred to the Eastern State Penitentiary in Philadelphia. There they would not have the freedoms and luxuries they had enjoyed at the county jail. From the state penitentiary they would be unable to run the family businesses or fulfill their duties as elected officials. They would most assuredly lose their connections to the outside.

"The worm has turned, Uncle Joe," commented Frank. "It's a Democratic world out there. They've made you, us, the scapegoats. There was bad blood on both sides, responsibility for the problems on both sides, but didn't our side, one of self-defense of home and family, seem obvious? Still they want to crucify us. They've gotten what they wanted, and now all they can see is that we're bad; we're the cause of all their problems. They refuse to admit all the good the Brunos have done for this town, for them as individuals. They just want us buried. Our friends either can't help us or won't—or they are no longer our friends."

Seven men in a jail cell is a bit of a crowd, but at that moment they were all very still, no one moving, no one speaking, each one almost holding his breath. They were all thankful that young Pauli had already been released from his ordeal.

Frank continued in a whisper, "We're alone up here on this mountain and it's crumbling."

Joseph glanced at Frank who looked so much like his father, Louis, so professional, usually so confident. But the long, drawn-out process had worn him down, too. Joseph suddenly remembered Louis calling him King of the Mountain when they were children and reflected on Frank's words.

Louis had said he would be Joseph's advisor, like Merlin in King Arthur's time. Never in his life had Joseph needed that advisor more.

"We have to get out," Joseph said quietly. The men had enjoyed much privacy in the jail—the warden had seen to that— but Joseph spoke softly now, almost as if he were praying.

"They're going to have to move us any day now, Papa." Fred said. "They can't keep putting it off. Someone's going to get wise to all this sooner or later."

They all knew the warden had put himself in jeopardy for them as long as he could. They knew they would be unable to stay in the county jail now that the trials were over.

Joseph nodded and said, "We will have to move quickly."

"I think you should go, Papa. Get out and find help," Jimmy said.

"No! If I leave, they'll come down hard on the rest of you!"

"Papa, you're the one they want to hang." Joseph winced at Fred's choice of words.

Fred noticed and changed his wording. "They want you in jail for the rest of your life. The rest of us are just gravy."

Joseph looked at Fred, then at Jimmy. Phil sat farther away, near the window, but turned to look at Joe when it got quiet.

Tony said, "You know I'll always do what you say, Uncle Joe."

"I can't leave you all behind!"

"You might have to, Papa," Jimmy said, laying his hand over his father's once-powerful one, now smaller somehow, almost frail, and without a doubt, older.

The whole long nightmare had worked on Jimmy's soul. Time is a great healer, they say, and now the people around him, his family, appeared much more important to him than a girl he had loved ten years ago. He wondered again, if he was coming to his senses too late. If he had supported his father all these years, would they perhaps not be in this place now?

Perhaps, he thought, *he and Fred should have taken over from the older generation sooner, but that was all water under the bridge. The important thing now was to figure out how to support his father in any way he could and where they could all go from here.*

CHAPTER 11

ESCAPE

On December 10, 1936, a little more than two years after the election eve massacre, Joseph, his sons, his brother and nephews were still being kept in relative comfort in the Schuylkill County Jail. But it couldn't last much longer—if they were going to make a break, it had to be now or never.

The Democrats were in complete control so all hope of appeals was over and at any moment the men could be transferred to the state penitentiary. They knew the accommodations would not be like those they had been enjoying at the Schuylkill County Jail. And the connections that Joseph had would never reach to Philadelphia and the state-run facility. Though Joseph and his lawyers had been able to delay the transfer to the state penitentiary several times, he knew that time was running out.

The debate about when Joseph should go now hinged on money. County officials had made several large payoffs to the Brunos in the previous two weeks totaling almost one hundred thousand dollars. Now it was a matter of transferring the money to Joseph at the jail—no easy task—but one which would be inconceivable at the state facility. Meanwhile, Antoinette was very busy moving the cash around and had formed a plan.

The men had hoped that all the family members would be able to escape together. But now there was just not enough time, so they had all decided to concentrate on Joseph's escape. They gathered around to finish the job of convincing him.

"You're the oldest …," Phil began.

"And the smartest," Fred added.

"And your health is not getting any better in here, Father," Alfred added.

"And the one with the longest imprisonment ahead of you," Frank continued. "Three life sentences, Uncle Joe. None of us can imagine you spending the rest of your life in jail, especially for something you did not do."

"You have the most connections, too," Phil said.

"But I can't leave you all here! I cannot imagine what will happen if I leave you all behind!"

"Don't imagine it. Think about getting out, getting help. You have to go, Papa," Fred knelt at his father's side, speaking softly, but earnestly. "It's not your decision to make by yourself anymore. We all want you to go. We need you to go."

Though Joseph saw the logic of their words, the pain it caused him was physical. To leave these men—his sons, his dear brother, his nephews—in the hands of an enemy who would be full of rage at his escape, was almost more than he could bear.

"Papa, you can't go to that prison. You couldn't stand it. You know that."

"And the rest of you can?"

"Yes, we can. We'll be all right. It will be hard for a little while, then things will settle down and life will go on. Antoinette will visit, and Mama, and we'll all write letters," Fred's voice trailed off as he spoke, barely convincing himself.

Jimmy spoke quietly, "We don't have any choice. We can't all get out, not now, not without more preparation. We don't have enough time, nor any more time to argue. You have to go. You have to do this for all of us, or we'll all be sent up. No one will get out."

"Go, Joe, you need to go," Phil said, his big hand which was always there protecting him, resting on his brother's shoulder. "Get help. Take care of us like you always have." He looked around at the close-knit family.

Joseph could not speak. He nodded to all of them, and forced himself to think of what had to happen next. No one knew for sure how long it would be before the county officials would run out of excuses and have to transfer the inmates to the penitentiary. Even to the family, all the trumped up delays had begun to look suspicious. Though Joseph dreaded leaving his family, he knew it had to be done if he was to find any help for them on the outside.

Joseph would need money—lots of it. Clearly, Antoinette would have to play a major role in the escape. Since the trials and incarceration, she had evolved, out of necessity, into the outside agent or gun moll, if you will. She had a natural ability for persuasion and timing, and instinctively knew the best methods by which to conduct the family business.

So the plans were made and the transfer of funds began immediately. Antoinette had to be clever as she made several visits to the bank within just a few days. She removed stocks and bonds from her father's safe deposit box—a large box, eight inches wide and six inches deep, and tightly crammed with all sorts of valuable papers. She made frequent visits to her father carrying the money. It was not really that difficult. When she visited the jail, the guards always managed to be busy, so she and her father would have all the privacy and time they needed

Over a two-week period, Antoinette delivered approximately fifty thousand dollars to her father. By the end of the following week, most of the money was hidden around Joseph's cell. The money had come from two county officials who had each provided almost twenty thousand dollars and she had sold several bonds and stocks as well.

On the morning of December 17, 1935, just a week before Christmas, Joseph told his daughter that he had to have at least five thousand dollars more by the next morning so he would be able to leave. Now that the time was at hand, Antoinette was fearful that the escape might not work as they had hoped. It had all seemed so simple when it was just a plan, but now, what if something went wrong?

Antoinette actually visited the jail four times that day, even returning in the late afternoon, which was unusual. She had only been able to bring three thousand dollars in her morning visit. She had to collect the other two thousand dollars from a local woman who was late with a payment. Antoinette had approached the woman twice before without success. This time she told her that she must pay immediately or there would be consequences. She spoke firmly to the woman. She didn't like to do that, but it was the only way to save her family. It was one of the responsibilities she had accepted to help her family.

Finally, the time arrived for the plan to unfold. Everything was set and waiting to be put into motion. No mistakes could occur. No detail could be left untouched.

Later that afternoon in December, Joseph walked into the administration office and told the office clerk, his son Jimmy, that he was having a relapse of the toothache that had plagued him earlier in the month. He asked Jimmy to make an appointment for first thing in the morning as he didn't know how much longer he could deal with the throbbing pain. Jimmy said he would set the appointment and notify the warden of the schedule for the next morning. Jimmy had scheduled many such appointments in the past two years for dentists, doctors, and lawyers. But this time was different.

The following morning, Joseph got out of a car on the corner of Second and Center Streets in downtown Pottsville. He leaned over before closing the door and said to the young guard, "Drive around and see if you can find a spot to park. Here, maybe you can find something special for your gal."

Joseph handed the young man a wad of bills, then turned and said over his shoulder, "Oh, and get us a cup of coffee, too. See you upstairs." And Joseph added politely, "Thank you!"

The driver was already thinking what he could buy for his girlfriend—after all it was only a week until Christmas. He hadn't made enough money this month to get a gift for her, or anyone else, for that matter. He was new on the job as a guard, and hadn't had time to save much. He knew just where to find that special present, something she had shown him in a shop window about three blocks away.

The young man smiled and waved, saying, "Yeah, thanks to you, too, Big Joe! Good luck! I'll see you upstairs!" He sped off as Joseph shut the car door and stepped up to the curb.

Joseph stood on the curb looking up and down Center Street. It was fairly busy for an early morning, but then again it was last minute Christmas shopping time, too. He started to look the other direction a second time, then decided it might make him appear suspicious. Instead, he started walking slowly and casually toward the meeting place. The joyful Christmas displays in the shop windows were tempting, and though he did not have time to waste, he tried to look like a holiday shopper. It was important not to attract attention. After all, he was an easily recognizable person throughout the county, especially after the events and trials of the last two years.

Joseph suddenly realized that his face would very soon become even more familiar, as he took yet another step toward becoming an escaped convict. As he headed eastward, he thought, *God, I hope everything is going as planned. Is everyone, everything in place?* He had no doubt Antoinette would be, but how about everyone else? The plan was complicated and everything had to be perfectly synchronized.

At the same time, Antoinette was standing on the corner of Third and Main, deep in her own thoughts. *I must be calm. I have been standing here for almost two hours, waiting for my part of this day, this important day, to begin. I arrived early so that if later any people remember me they would not be able to connect me to the time when the event took place.*

Now I must act quickly and flawlessly, so that no one can put me in the broader picture of this event. I'll wait in the doorway of this drugstore for just a few minutes more, looking at the Christmas display until I see the car approach. She felt her heart almost stop, then skip a few beats. *Now! Now! I cross the street to rendezvous with my father. I hand my father the last bundle of hundred dollar bills which I just received. I also give him the note from my mother and another envelope filled with papers—his new identity, his future.*

Joseph took the envelope from his daughter and climbed into the car. He opened the envelope to find his new identity papers. He would become a man named "Frank Miller," a man who traveled for his own business as an import-export tycoon. Joseph could speak Spanish as well as Italian as a result of dealing with the exporters of the cigar business and his employees in Spanish. His new business would be buying and selling imported goods from Latin America. "Frank Miller" was on his way to Cuba to buy and sell some products that very afternoon. His ticket was in the envelope and he had connections in Cuba from the cigar business the family had owned for years.

Joseph had started his adventure. He went first to Tamaqua with an old friend who was driving the first car. When they got to Tamaqua, there was no time for good-byes. He rushed to a second car, which stood waiting. That car carried him to a small airfield where he boarded a plane. The plane, bound for Miami, took off immediately with Joseph as its sole passenger.

Once in Miami, Joseph boarded a commercial plane for Havana. As he took his seat, he glanced at his watch and realized that it had been only six hours since he had left the jail. Only when the plane was airborne, when he was completely off American soil, did he feel safe.

Joseph spent several days in Havana where he posed as a cigar inspector and was well-looked after by his business associates and friends who played along and kept "Frank" busy and unnoticed. The carefully orchestrated plan continued to unfold as the third day came and Joseph was driven to the Havana airport to return to the United States.

The timing of the return was critical, as by then the warden would be issuing a national alarm that Joseph Bruno, a man serving three life sentences, had walked away from the Schuylkill County Jail in Pennsylvania. Because he would be departing from Havana, Joseph would have the element of surprise to cloak his return to the United States via New York City. Those who had purchased the tickets for him using a

"Frank Miller" passport, had also purchased tickets for flights to Denver and Chicago, hoping that these false trails would lead his pursuers in the wrong directions, and make it unlikely that they would search for Joseph in New York City. The family had made the assumption that law enforcement would be expecting Joseph to take a flight to Italy, not be reentering the country. Thus the FBI would be watching the departing flights, not the arrivals.

Finally Joseph was safe; but what was that to him now, alone in New York City? Actually alone for the first time in his life. He had always had his family around him—parents, sisters and brothers, uncles, aunts, cousins. Then, later, his beloved Cecilia and their children, nephews, nieces, grandchildren. Now he was alone with a price on his head, an escaped convict who had been accused of the most horrendous crimes and sentenced to spend the rest of his life in prison.

But there was no time for fear, no time for grief. He had been trained well by his father to be strong, to stand up to his fate like a man, shoulders back, chest out. He was a Bruno, Joseph James Bruno—proud of his name and determined to clear it. He had no time to waste in useless recrimination. He had a job to do.

Meanwhile, Joseph's absence had been discovered back at the county jail. Several of the officers were suspected of aiding in his escape. How could they not have known what was taking place under their own noses?

The guard that accompanied Joseph to the dentist had been handpicked by Joseph, not the warden. He had only recently been appointed as a guard at the facility, replacing, for some unknown reason, the previous guard who had been given early retirement. A guard so young and inexperienced should not have been escorting a prisoner to town. If he had been issued a weapon, he did not have it with him that morning, nor had he been fully trained in how to use one.

In addition, he was using his own car and did not have another guard accompanying him. The idea of using his own car and not a county vehicle was so as not to draw attention to them in town when Joseph was left off at the curb. The county jail officials would certainly not have chosen such a man.

Antoinette was arrested and taken to the county courthouse for questioning that evening. She was arraigned that night on six charges, including negligence, accessory after the fact of murder, conspiracy to aid an escape, taking money into a prison for her father, assisting and comforting an escaped prisoner, and bribery. She was held incommunicado, not even allowed to speak with her mother.

Antoinette's arrest took place on a Saturday and, since the bondsmen were not open on Sunday, was not released until Monday after twelve grueling hours of questioning. She was able to secure the fifteen thousand dollars bail by mortgaging a piece of property which her father had recently put it in her name.

Some of the prison officials were charged with gross negligence, conspiracy and willfully allowing a prisoner to escape. The guard who escorted Joseph to the dentist was arrested and held for fifteen thousand dollars bail as well. After numerous witnesses and prisoners of the jail were questioned, all the prison employees being held, including the young guard, were released on bail. Bail for these people was paid by mysterious means. For most of them, like the guard, did not have that kind of money or collateral.

An investigation of the escape highlighted several unusual circumstances surrounding the Bruno family's incarceration. First of all, Joseph, his brother, and their sons had all been made trustees of the county jail several weeks prior to their incarceration. Thus they were able to control many of the functions and most of the administration of the facility.

When investigators went to the jail they found Joseph's now-empty cell locked. Joseph had carried the key to his suite and only locked the doors when he was not inside, assuring that his belongings would not go missing. Joseph could roam freely in the halls of the jail and many times could be found in the administration offices using the telephone or listening to the radio.

Cell number 12, Joseph's temporary home, contained furniture from his home, including a bed, a wardrobe that held his suits and coats, a matching dresser filled with freshly pressed and laundered shirts, individually folded and wrapped, with light starch, and, by the door, a hat rack holding three fedoras.

His cell was stocked with sheets, blankets, a bedspread and pillows, also from his home. Curtains covered the windows and bars on the doorway, providing privacy and blocking the light from the hall. Joseph had been ill in the recent past and was always napping. The bright light from the hall bothered him. There was also a coffee table and two chairs in the adjoining cell, for receiving the many people who came to visit him and for those who came to conduct business.

The cell next to his served as the family's dining room, furnished with plates and tableware with the Bruno initials. Cabinets were stocked with caviar, paté de fois gras, and many imported specialty foods. Both rooms had carpets on the floor for insulation against the cold and damp. As a final touch, pictures were hung on the walls to lend a more comfortable atmosphere.

The other members of the family had similar comforts in their cells. All the men had trunks for their belongings like those used by well-to-do passengers on cruise ships, all packed with their pressed shirts and accessories.

Joseph and his family had access to the kitchen, so they could cook food brought to them by visitors. They rarely ate anything that was made by the jail kitchen staff. They even cooked their own breakfasts and ate together in the privacy of their dining room.

Many afternoons, the air of the jailhouse was filled with the aroma of frying sausage, peppers, and homemade sauce. On occasion there was even wine available to accompany dinner, and occasionally, some other inmates were invited to eat with the family members being detained in the jailhouse.

Regular inmates, who were required to work and be at their positions by seven o'clock in the morning, were told on more than a few mornings to be quiet when entering the cellblock because Joseph Bruno slept until nine. Joseph had obtained the job of assistant to the prison doctor, which afforded him a leisurely schedule as the doctor rarely needed an assistant.

Joseph's sons and brother also had jobs at the jail. Philip was the operator of the commissary and brought in new items. He controlled the newspaper and cigarette trade, as well as the barbershop, where he raised the prices. In this way he was able to run the shop at a profit from which he benefited.

Jimmy was in charge of the administration office as head clerk. The office was actually located at the entrance to the jail, not within the secured areas, and all the keys to the cells as well as the entire facility were kept in that office. The area also housed the cabinets where the jailers kept their weapons when off duty. As clerk, Jimmy had access to all keys and areas of top security as well as the files and important papers which arrived and flowed through the office of the prison. Many of these papers pertained to confidential matters of security at the jail.

In addition, Jimmy had easy access to the outside doors of the jail and could easily have walked out on numerous occasions. The ledger for visitors, which was also kept there, showed that Bruno family members were allowed to visit the prisoners almost at will. The family had visitors at all hours, some of whom were political. Most of the teachers from the schools visited. Often the visits were leisurely, and several actually occurred in the administrative office with the door closed for privacy.

Joseph always had a large supply of the finest cigars which he smoked and enjoyed freely, products of the cigar factory he owned in Hazleton that had continued to roll cigars for sale in New York City and along the East Coast.

The investigation also uncovered that many of the visits to the Brunos were not even recorded in the ledger. All the visitor had to do was tell the guard or Jimmy that he or she was a friend of Joe's, and the visitor could walk right in. On the day before the escape, when Antoinette had visited four times, only one visit was logged. The ledger also showed that the other imprisoned family members had come and gone from the jail to doctors and dentists throughout their confinements.

Joseph had managed his business affairs from the jail almost as before. He supervised the gambling and vice ring that had handled more than two million dollars over the previous ten years, as well as the vice payoff operation, which ran into hundreds of thousands of dollars.

Investigators were appalled to discover the freedom that the Bruno family members had enjoyed. No one seemed to realize that the men could have escaped at any time, or done serious damage, had they been so inclined, but they did not. The prisoners believed they were innocent, and that justice would prevail. They were confident that the truth of their innocence would be shown through proper legal channels.

The day following the escape, while she was being detained at the courthouse for questioning, Antoinette stood at the window of the district attorney's office. From there she saw her uncle Philip, her brothers Fred and Jimmy, and her cousins Anthony and Arthur being led out of the county jail to the State Department of Corrections transfer bus.

For Antoinette, that was the most awful moment of her experience. Everything she knew of and had dreamed of as a young girl was gone, loaded onto a prison bus. A nightmare had been unleashed that November election eve two years earlier; a nightmare that was worsening each day. Not only were the men in her life being taken away to the state penitentiary, but, even more devastating for Antoinette, was that her father was on the run and she had no idea where he was, or when she would see or hear from him again.

Suddenly, Arthur looked up at the window and saw Antoinette standing there. He waved goodbye, blowing a kiss to the wind. Her whole family was being destroyed, her world turned upside down, and, as she stood there, everything began to spin in her mind, dizzying and disorienting her so that she fell to the floor in a faint. Antoinette woke to see a guard bending over her. Outside her brothers and other family members were gone. She felt guilty for letting them down, felt she needed to be stronger, and instantly vowed to continue the struggle for her family's freedom and survival.

When Antoinette was finally released, she left the room with her cousin and went into the corridor where her youngest brother

Ernest sat waiting for her. She smiled in relief—she still had innocent young Ernie! She felt so much joy in seeing him and holding him in her arms that she never wanted to let him go.

Ernie laughed and struggled to release himself. He was only seventeen and had been away at boarding school when the event occurred. That night had left him the only male in the family who had not had his whole life destroyed, outwardly, that is.

Ernie felt guilty for not having been there and for being the only one in the family who was free. He was tormented by so many emotions, but he felt it was up to him to take care of the family. He was home for the holidays and had been sitting in the corridor for hours while his sister was questioned. He was unknown to most people in town and could go about pretty much unnoticed. He had overheard numerous conversations about his father and brothers, most of which were unkind. He felt sorry for his sister and thought it unfair that she was being treated as a criminal. After all, she had only tried to help their father, something he felt unable to do. Only a few days earlier, Antoinette came to the school to take him home for Christmas vacation in time to visit his father at the jail. She was a wonderful, caring sister who had to bear so much—it was simply not fair.

Late that afternoon the transfer bus with its load of five new prisoners arrived at the Eastern State Penitentiary located on Cherry Hill in the Fairmont district of Philadelphia. The prisoners were to be known from that day on as D–1814, D–1815, D–1816, D–1817 and D–1818 and treated as ordinary prisoners.

The five men were led inside to Block 14, where they were each issued a prison uniform of blue striped denim and a pair of heavy black work shoes. The men were used to the best wools, silks, and linens; not the cheap, common state-issued uniforms. But the well-tailored suits, elegant shoes and all personal valuables were taken and put into storage pending the release of the prisoners.

Next, the men were taken to the showers where they had to strip and be searched. They were given prison soap made from lye, guaranteed to rid all prisoners of any lice and germs and ordered to shower. After the humiliating showers and searches, they were taken to the prison barber, where they received the usual prison haircut—a shaved head. All those experience were most degrading, yet they were forced to endure every one.

The cells they were led to contained common metal bunks with prison mattresses and sparse furnishings. They would remain in the holding area during a quarantine period of thirty days. Their meals would be served in their cells, and they would be allowed no visitors during the quarantine. They would only be permitted to exercise in the courtyard at times when no other prisoners were there.

The world was a new one to all of them, one they could never have imagined before that day. But they knew they would have to grow used to it in order to survive. They were happy that Joseph had escaped before being sent here. They firmly believed he would not have been able to handle such humiliation.

Life for the Bruno family both inside and outside the penitentiary was made a little more bearable knowing that Joseph was free and somewhere out there trying to establish a new defense. Whenever they felt low, they imagined him eating an Italian meal or walking along a city street enjoying his freedom and looking forward to theirs.

CHAPTER 12

PRISON

Entries from Antoinette Bruno's diary.

December 21, 1936 –

Thank God the holidays are over. How could we even celebrate Christmas this year? We were finally able to return to the church; but now that Papa has escaped, the town is treating us badly again. I would have loved to listen to the music at the midnight mass. To be kept out of our own church! It's criminal! The very church my grandfather and his brother helped build. And to think of all the money my family has poured into that church over the years.

I've told Mama not to read the papers. It's unbelievable what they say! Papa skipped out and left the others to their fate. Imagine! His own brother and sons and nephews! How stupid to think that a man like my father would do that.

January 1, 1937 –

A new year. What will it hold? It will have to be better—it can't be worse. Papa had to sell some of the property he owned in Hazleton before he left the jail. The costs of the trials and appeals is staggering.

Thank the Lord we still have some of the business money coming in.

January 9, 1937 –

It has been weeks since the escape and we have no news of Papa. I pray every night and every morning that he is safe, that he is all right. Oh, dear God, please take care of him! He's not well, he needs us. He's not used to being alone, without his family. God, please protect him.

January 13, 1937 –

Finally! Mama got word today that he is safe and back in America! Oh, thank you, God, thank you! She doesn't know where he is or how and when he got there. We only know that he misses us and that he is well. And now I have a part again. He needs me to take him important information and some more money.

In the middle of January, 1937, after the quarantine period was over, Antoinette went to the state penitentiary for her first visit. She had been waiting impatiently to go. Her mother wanted to see her boys, but it was a long, difficult journey to Philadelphia, and they could not be sure of what they would find.

How would her sons look? Had they been eating right? Were they healthy? Had they been changed into unrecognizable men, older than their years? Cecilia could not make the difficult journey and then be driven to despair by not being able to do anything to help.

So the family decided that Antoinette would go alone. She had her father's strong will. Since the day they had left the county jail, she had become another person, stronger than one would have guessed with her petite frame.

Antoinette had locked her feelings away deep inside. She only let them out when the lights were off and she was alone in her bedroom. Occasionally, her sister or younger brother would hear her sobbing in the middle of the night. She tried to stifle the sounds of her sobs in her pillow, but many times they could still hear her. They never told either Antoinette or their mother; it would only undermine their resolve.

When Antoinette arrived at the penitentiary, she stood for several minutes looking at the fortress-like building where some of her family now lived. She could not believe how cold and lifeless the place looked. How could it be any better on the inside?

Antoinette knew she had to be brave and keep her emotions under control, even though she felt she was dying inside. She took a deep breath, like a true Bruno, held her head high and with her chest out proudly, walked right through the front gates and into that bleak hell.

The situation was worse than she ever could have imagined. There was no sign of human kindness, of comfort, or of hope. It was a place of complete despair, but she kept walking. As she walked toward the visitors' window, she felt as if she were floating. As she moved, a vision of the whole horrible stream of events that led her to this cold, heartless place whirled in her head. She registered as Antoinette Bruno, sister, cousin and niece of the five prisoners whose numbers she could not bear to acknowledge.

Once registered, she had to wait for what seemed like hours in the cold and friendless waiting area. Finally she was called forward. She stood tall and walked to the visitation room where she almost lost her composure. Facing her was a narrow room, nothing more than two bare-walled corridors, with stark wooden benches for seats and a wall of glass meshed with wire separating the two sides. The other side was almost identical and empty except for a guard standing at the far end. The expressionless man who led her in motioned for her to sit on one of the benches, then stepped back two or so feet behind her with his arms crossed over his chest, still without a trace of emotion.

The guard stared down at her, actually looking as if he thought he was superior to her. An uneducated roughneck guard, superior to her! She thought, then a smile came over her as she looked at him a second time. She informed him she would be speaking Italian, and if he needed any help translating, she would be happy to help. She spoke such elegant English that the guard was taken aback by her genuine superiority.

Antoinette stared at him, then looked down the corridor at the other guard, waiting and wondering what would happen next.

Just as a wave of total helplessness and anxiety began to flow over her body, a door on the other side opened suddenly with a clang. Through the cold steel door marched her brother Jimmy. In spite of her firm control, a single tear rolled down her cheek and splashed upon the hard cement floor. But it was the only tear she allowed to escape that day.

Antoinette spoke to her relatives one at a time, first to Jimmy, then to Fred. She felt she did not have enough time with either one. She had so much she wanted to say and so much to deliver from Mama. But the time passed too quickly.

"I'll come back as soon as they allow me to—I swear it!" Antoinette told her brothers. "I'll bring Mama with me."

"Jimmy," she said, "you must uphold the proud Bruno name while Mama is here. You must not give her the tiniest glimpse of the difficult life you are being forced to live." She repeated her words to Fred. Each of the men nodded, knowing she understood how it was for them, and not wanting to add to the already heavy load their mother was bearing.

Antoinette also met with her cousins and uncle for a few minutes each before she was told she had to leave. She was only able to give them messages and receive others from them for their loved ones at home.

No one mentioned her father, but from gestures and between the lines they learned from her that he was still free and she knew where he was. Knowing that gave them strength. She asked them all to look after one another and to remain strong. It seemed to her that each of her brothers and the others left the room with a little more stature and pride in their walk.

Antoinette survived the visit to the prison, an experience she had never dreamed would be a part of her life. Once she was back in the taxi, she cried from helplessness, exhaustion and a total lack of hope. She cried so long and hard that she could not tell the driver which platform she needed at the station. Finally, she handed him her ticket and he pointed her to the correct platform. She went into the station walking as proud and as tall as she had when she first arrived. The only thing she could think of to do was to survive, so that soon, somehow, she could see her father again.

When Antoinette returned home, she showed no outward signs of despair. She gave no indication that her kinsmen's life in the prison was probably hell on earth. She gave glorious accounts of their individual welfare to all the relatives who came to call. She delivered the messages to their loved ones and received still more messages for her next visit. She hid her tears and her fears for her brothers behind a curtain of hope. She realized it was just a matter of time until her mother would insist on seeing her sons.

January 24, 1937 –

I'm going to see my father! I can hardly wait to be wrapped in his warm bear hug, to be called his little Antoinette Marie. Yet I am anxious and afraid, too. I have a secret bag of things for him; but the thing I want most is to see my dear papa.

I constantly ask, how did life go so bad? How did it get so hard? Some say it's all those things that the family did through the years— the gambling, the women, the payoffs. They say it's wrong. Is it? Was it always wrong? Is it only wrong now because we got caught? Where are all those people who were involved—all those politicians getting their share? All we see now is their backs!

I do know that what Papa and Jimmy and Fred and the others did that night to protect us wasn't wrong! The other people were dangerous! They had threatened us! Believe me; I was there.

The testimony that came out about that night was totally false; not a shred of truth in it. The people were not marching in a parade. They were behaving like a mob. Our house was quiet, and we were going about our business. When the first shots were fired from across the street, I was inside the house and I saw my father try to stop the shooting. He even went outside to plead to the mob, but they booed him.

Aunt Margaret is with us a lot now. She can't bear to be home alone. She comes and sits quietly only going home when she is so tired she knows she will go right to sleep. Her company is good for Mama. What a sad world we live in. Is this really what God meant for us?

February 4, 1937 –

I saw my father—finally! But such a journey I had to take! I want to write it down, before I forget, but I can't keep it. I'll have to burn the paper so they won't find him!

I start by going to Allentown carrying a large carpetbag so full of goodies I can hardly lift it. Mama has prepared all of Papa's favorite foods. Each of us has written a letter.

In Allentown, I switch to a private car that my cousin Pauli drives. He drives as if he were in a funeral procession. He tells me that he does not want to draw attention as we drive through the Lehigh Valley to Easton. If I weren't so scared, I'd be giggling, riding in the back seat like a queen!

At Easton I meet my cousin Franco, who escorts me as my beau on the train to Newark. In Newark, I finally get to rest. We stop to eat at a small deli that Uncle Pauli's nephew, Antonio, owns. So many people are coming and going, no one will remember seeing me.

Franco tells me that another family friend is going to meet me nearby in fifteen minutes. I am to embrace the stranger, for he is to act as my husband for the rest of the journey. I must say he is the most handsome husband I could hope for. He looks like Frank Sinatra and speaks fluent Italian. As he gives me a warm greeting and a firm hug anyone would believe we were married. I have to compose my feelings as I remind myself this is a theatrical performance by a total stranger who is on my father's payroll.

I am whisked into a waiting cab. The driver addresses me by my name and explains that he is a friend of the family. He asks if I am comfortable. Before I can reply, my "husband" politely apologizes for his liberal behavior earlier. His name is Luigi Abetto, a distant cousin related through my grandmother. His father owes their family fortunes to my grandfather.

I will stop now, read this over and memorize it. Then I will throw it into the coal fire burning in my room.

February 5, 1937 –

I had a busy day today and I'm tired, but I must write some more so I won't forget anything.

When we arrive at the entrance to the Holland Tunnel the tollbooth worker smiles and wishes us a pleasant evening.

"The sun will soon be rising so take care," he adds. "Move quickly in the tunnel as there will be little time to spare."

"What did he mean?" I ask Luigi as we enter the long tube.

"As soon as I tell you, you must jump out of that door and into the next car," Luigi said, pointing to a vehicle approaching on the left.

"Now!" he yells, and flings open my door as the two cars are side by side, still moving. As I jump, Luigi grabs my bag and follows on my heels. We tumble into the other car, barely touching the pavement. I gasp for breath and try to calm my pounding heart as the car speeds forward. I am glad they are taking such precautions, but I fear I may not survive the trip!

A moment later, I look at Luigi, then turn and look behind us. Once again, Luigi asks forgiveness for his necessary use of force and moves away.

Several hours of twisting and turning, changing vehicles, and moving secretively have passed and we our only now coming out the Manhattan exit of the Holland Tunnel.

"The tunnel was being watched," Luigi explained. "So we had to exit in a different car. The tunnel guard is a man who also owes much of his existence to your family."

I must remember my father is the object of the biggest manhunt in Pennsylvania history. So when they boss me around they are trying to protect him as well as themselves.

February 8 1937 –

Today I took Mama to the prison to see my uncles and brothers and cousin, so I am very tired and sad. Seeing my family there is so hard. It was especially hard to see the effect that it had on Mama. She held up well as long as she could, but I put her to bed as soon as we got back. Elveda made dinner tonight, and the girls helped by taking a small plate up to their nonna. I am so glad to be living here with my girls and Mama. All I want to do right now is crawl into bed but I must write some more for just a few minutes while I wait for the fire to burn down.

The tollbooth operator was right. The sun is about to rise over the East River. After we take two subways we arrive in Little Italy. We hurriedly walk several blocks and my husband leads me into a little café where we meet a woman who greets us kindly. Once inside, she closes the curtains and points to the kitchen door. In the kitchen stands a short Sicilian man chopping spinach for a fritatta. When we enter he drops the knife and starts to explain what happens next.

I am already weary, wondering how long it will be before I finally see my father. The man smiles at me kindly as if he understands, and in a Sicilian dialect reminiscent of my grandmother, explains that he will take me to an apartment upstairs where Luigi and I can freshen up and wait for further instructions.

"I need to see my father now!" I protest. "I will have plenty of time to pull myself together later!"

"I know you are tired and distraught from all you have been through. But this is so important we cannot be too careful. You understand, don't you?"

I nod. Nothing is more important than my father's safety. We have to wait a few more hours while my father is moved to another location so we would not know where he was actually hiding.

Luigi and I have some awkward moments once in the apartment. I go directly to the washroom so that I can wash some of the day's grime from my face and hands, and soak my feet in a basin of warm water. Luigi seems more interested in eating and discovers that the short Sicilian man knew what he was doing with those knives. A fresh-out-of-the-oven spinach and cheese fritatta is waiting on the table in the dining area of the small apartment kitchen, with two place settings, plenty of freshly baked bread, and strong Sicilian coffee. Luigi calls to me to join him, but my feet are too comfortable soaking and my mind is too comfortable wandering.

I am dreaming of what it will be like to see my father and wondering when it will ever happen. Besides, it is impossible for me to even consider food at this hour.

February 9, 1937 –

Today was a quiet peaceful day at home. I walked the girls to school and did the shopping. At least school is back to near normal although most of the teachers are new. People in town know what's done is done, and most feel the verdict was wrong. The Democrat leaders are getting their fill of disappointed constituents as they try to control a not-so-easy population of immigrant citizens. The majority of the population is so accustomed to receiving the help they were getting from Papa that they will never forgive the Democrats. The whole region is in dire straits. Now there is hunger and repossessions, the mines are letting the men go and the railroad is losing its importance without the working mines. People are actually looking back at the better times of Republican prosperity.

February 10, 1937 –

We baked the week's bread and made some sauce. Now I can sit down and finish my story.

After what seems like a few minutes, there's a knock at the washroom door and the friendly voice of the man asking if I am ready to continue my trip. I jump up, half spilling the basin of water as I realize I have probably been sleeping for several hours out of complete exhaustion. As I pull myself together and clean up the water, I shout, "Give me two minutes, no more!"

When I come out I see that Luigi has been asleep on the couch. I wonder how long he will continue to accompany me. Will he go back with me, too? Then he tells me that he has to return soon to his real family in Jersey. Then we are off again immediately and I do not have time to dwell on my own loneliness.

We are taken to the back of the apartment, to a fire escape that leads to the roof in the rear of the building. The street in front of the café is barely visible. For anyone to see us climbing onto the roof of the building behind is nearly impossible. We open a door that is more like a cellar trap door, and climb down a long ladder into what appears to be a pasta factory. There are huge bags of flour everywhere, and there is a gentle dusting of off-white flour floating around the huge room, making me think that magical beings are hiding in there, ready to conjure a miracle.

We quickly leave the huge warehouse by way of a loading dock that is covered with large crates of finished pasta of various types, and slip into an adjoining butcher shop. We are then rushed up several more flights of stairs and over the roof of a little Italian bakery on Mulberry Street.

Then for the first time in several weeks, I see my father. He is waiting just inside the storage room above the bakery.

February 11, 1937 –

Even though I had a peaceful day yesterday I still fell asleep over my writing. I jumped up when I woke and hastily tossed the pages into the fire. I must be more careful! It is foolish to write this but I feel I must.

The time Papa and I were able to spend together was so special. I am the only one to see him in weeks. I had so much to tell him, I wanted to stay for days. I knew that it was too dangerous and that I was only allowed a short visit.

February 12, 1937 –

Tomorrow morning I am going for another journey very early. I must say no more. I will write when I return.

February 16, 1937 –

I spent three days in Philadelphia supposedly shopping. I had the same type of experience as before, this time staying at a hotel there. The first night I actually slept in the room, although I tossed and turned most of the night. The next day, at perhaps four in the morning, I left for N.Y.C. to see Papa once again. Of course it was another maze of secret connections and evading any followers. It was worth it; he looked much better this time, but I can tell he is not happy and dealing with his ailment is difficult for him.

February 18, 1937 –

Mama wants me to take some important papers to Papa so that she can sign the lots in Haddock over to Elveda and me, to protect them from the courts. Papa already transferred most of his accounts to his sons, before the sentencing ever came down.

I am taking my daughter Celia with me as it will do Papa good to see his grandchild, and it is a good cover for the trip following so close behind my last one. I am supposedly taking Celia to see a specialist in Hartford, Connecticut.

February 25, 1937 –

Today a man came to the house saying he was just passing through. His excuse struck me as odd for no one ever just passes through Kelayres. He started asking so many questions, claiming to be Papa's friend from Detroit. When Mama and I went in the kitchen to make some coffee, I asked her if she had ever heard Papa speak of the man. She had no memory of ever meeting the stranger or hearing his name. Mama was simply content to have someone besides Aunt Margaret with whom she could enjoy a cup of espresso. She did not need a reason or explanation. The conversation and company was more than fulfilling for her. I decided to play along. After all, he was just passing through.

February 27, 1937 –

Well Mama's new friend is still here; he has taken a room in McAdoo. So much for passing through. I can't wait to see Papa, to ask if he knows the man. I really don't trust him and I told Mama not to either. She just shrugs her shoulders and tells me I am distrustful since everything happened, and I must accept things for what they are, not what they seem.

February 28, 1937 –

I cannot stop thinking of my Papa, praying for him, hoping that he will be all right. Will he have any luck finding help in the city? So many people have already helped us: all those who are helping me visit him and others who continue to work for the family businesses and get money to us. But no one can help get the men out of jail, get their verdicts changed or their sentences overturned. We need someone very powerful to do that. And all the men in power now are Democrats.

Sometimes I wonder if Papa is not in prison, too, even though he is not behind bars, even though he is living somewhere in New York City. To be in exile, kept away by fear from the family he loves, is that not a prison?

March 8, 1937 –

We have been so busy. I relentlessly keep tending to Papa's business collections and meet with his area supervisors often. It keeps the money coming in so the family can survive. Mama willingly minds the girls now, and they keep her occupied on the long, seemingly endless days.

That man keeps coming by to visit. I still don't trust him. He talks too much and seems to be searching for answers.

March 15, 1937 –

I've been to see my brothers several more times. It is an effort to go only to be surrounded by the stillness, lifelessness, and loneliness of that dreadful place. Seeing my brothers, however, is never an effort. I live for those too few and too brief moments. I just shut off my view of the surroundings and try to imagine being somewhere else. My favorite imaginary place is the Kelayres ballfield where we could breathe fresh mountain air and feel a cool breeze.

Because everything in the prison is the same day after day, I know that I am the only distraction in their mundane existence. That is why I try so hard to lift them above their depressing surroundings with good news and letters from loved ones.

Today I tell them that Frank is working relentlessly to get them pardons. There are some connections in the state courts now with new appointments that may be fruitful. Hopefully we will hear any day now, and their existence in the prison will be just an ugly memory.

March 21, 1937 –

I feel a deep bond developing between my father and me. It means so much to me to be the one to see him, to help him in this awful time. And I feel strongly that I must clear his name. Papa said he does not

*know the stranger from Detroit! We must be careful, and not let him
know we know that he is lying.*

April 15, 1937 –

*Another blow to our family came today. The director of schools
changed the name of the new school. It's now the Kelayres School.*

*But erasing everything that the Bruno name means in this town
is not that easy. Even though they've changed the name, "Bruno
School" is still written on the lintel above the front entrance. And it
will always be there. It's carved in stone.*

April 20, 1937 –

*God bless us all, Arthur and Anthony are being released with
pardons today! Aunt Margaret and Mama prepared a special feast
for tonight. I am waiting now to meet them as free men, so I must
go. The paperwork is endless. I pray they will walk through that door
any minute.*

April 22, 1937 –

*It is so good to have Arthur and Anthony home. Mama is like a
young girl again. She senses a time when Papa will be home, too.*

April 27, 1937 –

*I went to court again today, and hallelujah! All charges against
me were dropped! Nothing could be proven, so they had to drop all
claims. I think the tide is finally turning in the family's favor.
I pray it is so.*

*Frank was a dear, and has been all along. I don't know what
we would have done without him. I think it helped him, too, to
have something go right for a change. All these trials and court
appearances have cost us a fortune. I'm glad some of that money
stayed in the family!*

Joseph was growing more tired and lonely in his self-appointed
exile. His family meant so much to him. His health, already
weakening before the tragedy, had been further undermined by
the trials, the time in jail, and the lonely escape and months in
hiding.

Cecilia also had experienced much grief. Still she carried on with her head held high. Joseph had taught his children the same:

"Never let anyone look down on you. Always keep yourself above them so that you are admired and respected no matter what may happen." Although Joseph was suffering from the loneliness and shame that he must bear, he continued to send the family words of encouragement and uplifting thoughts in his letters home.

The notes and letters family members exchanged were always handwritten and sent back and forth by a variety of means. The letters would have to be smuggled into their homes or back to New York City by any number of messengers, only one of whom was Antoinette. She could not count how many trips she made to see her father. It only mattered that she saw him as often as possible, though even then it was never enough. It was so dangerous and so long and tiring, but it was always worth it when she saw her father's eyes sparkle.

While Antoinette may not have seen a great deal of her father, she saw a great deal of New York City, more than she ever imagined she would with all the maneuvering, hiding, and running around. Nor did she ever see the place where her father stayed and, as she found out later, never even went anywhere near his neighborhood. At some point, Antoinette found out that he had lived at 202 East 75th Street, on the Upper East Side. The apartment was a small walk-up on the third floor holding a twin bed, a few furnishings, and photos of the family to brighten it up. Joseph spent most of his time on his two favorite pastimes—reading and listening to music, especially opera.

Sometimes, late at night while alone in her own room, Antoinette, strong Antoinette, who never cried but always held her head high, let her tears flow and her pain break free. On one of those nights, before she even realized it, her mother was holding her, comforting her, talking softly to her.

"Ah, Mama, I'm so sorry, I never meant to bother you, to waken you," Antoinette sobbed.

"Hush, child, it's nothing, you are my daughter, you have been so strong for all of us. Now I will be strong for you." And Cecilia held her daughter as she had years ago, when Antoinette was a little girl.

"Do you remember, during the war, when you wanted to do something important, something useful, like the boys? Well, my dear, you are doing that now. The men are helpless, locked away, gone—they need us now more than they ever have. We are not alone though. We have each other, you and I. We still have the *capos* and our friends in New York. And some of your papa's workers are still here."

Antoinette looked at her mother in amazement, surprised that she knew so much, that she was talking about things that her father had told her never to discuss with her mother.

Cecilia smiled, knowing what was in her daughter's mind.

"Everything is different now, my dear. We have always been strong, but now we can admit to it. We must carry on. Your own daughters look to you for strength, for guidance."

At times like that Antoinette would think of her grandparents, Nonna Marie Antonia, and Nonno James. They had always been so proud of what they had accomplished in America. Thank the Lord they had never had to deal with any of this horror. What would they do if they were here now? They would stiffen up and walk proud as peacocks, just as her mama was telling her now.

May 6, 1937 —

We have been so busy with the pardons and appeals that I have not had a moment to write. The news is bad once again, the tide has not turned after all. My brothers' pardons were denied again. The appeal is being written again. Why is it so difficult to see that an injustice has been done? Thank God, Arthur and Anthony got out.

June 8, 1937 —

I knew that man was not to be trusted! Mama kept feeding him and letting him visit, even after I told her Papa didn't know him.

He befriended her, but I never gave in to his trickery. Well, he followed me all the way into Philadelphia on my last trip. So I had to abort seeing Papa and actually shop in the city and head back home, having accomplished nothing except for getting some new clothes.

Of course when he realized that I saw him snooping behind me, he had an excuse for being in the city too, and wasn't it a wonderful coincidence? Now that we ran into each other, he could buy me lunch, and we could ride the train back together. Oh what horror! It was bad enough not to be able to see Papa, but to have to eat with this man and spend the whole afternoon together on a train was pure torture!

I told Mama as soon as I got into the house and away from his presence. The incident proves he is not to be trusted, but we must carry on as if we don't suspect a thing. We must be careful not to raise his suspicions of us. If he knows we suspect him, then he'll know we have contact with Papa. That would give everything away.

CHAPTER 13

RECAPTURED

On the morning of August 23, 1937, the temperature in New York City was already sweltering. But Joseph Bruno, walking down the sidewalk of East 76th Street, was carefully dressed with a fedora and new wire-rimmed glasses, both placed perfectly upon his head, stepping tall and proud, as always. His face had aged more than his fifty-five years, and his body pained him, but his spirit remained unbroken. Joseph had grown a mustache, dyed his hair black, and gained some weight.

Joseph saw two men cross the street at the light at the corner. He thought he recognized one as his old friend and colleague, Louis Buono. He glanced their way again, then saw a little neighbor boy playing on the sidewalk. He smiled at the child and gave him a shiny new half dollar. Then he looked a third time. It was Louis, with another man from his hometown. Joseph continued walking toward them.

When he was only a few steps away, Joseph turned to the men and said in Italian, "Good morning, Louis," just as he would have done on a normal morning in Kelayres or Hazleton. As they walked by, Louis thought he heard a familiar voice. He hesitated, furrowed his brow and pondered what he thought he heard.

230 • BRUCE BOYD

Louis turned quickly to see his old friend, now his nemesis, Joseph Bruno. He recognized Joseph's distinguished peacock-like stride and wondered how he could have missed it.

"I am ready to go home now, Louis," Joseph said, already face-to-face with him. "I did nothing wrong. Everything was twisted to make me look guilty. And I am sorry for the pain and hardship I have caused my family."

"Come on then, Joe. It's time to go," Louis said.

"I *want* to go," said Joseph. So Big Joe Bruno joined the two men and they all walked off together as the little boy on the sidewalk stood staring at his shiny new coin.

At 2:30 PM, Joseph was booked as a fugitive at the East 67th Street Station of the New York City police. Joseph was held overnight by the police for lineup and questioning, then was told they would begin to file papers for his extradition to Pennsylvania.

The police searched his apartment, wondering among themselves where he had been for nearly eight months. How had he been able to hide himself so well? The police needed to find evidence that someone had helped him, or that he had been receiving correspondence over the time period. They hoped to find money in the apartment that had allowed him to eat and clothe himself so fashionably. They found nine dollars in his pocket and one hundred and nine dollars in his shoe. But they found nothing else. Not a clue as to where Joseph may have gone during the long search for one of Pennsylvania's most wanted fugitives. Not a record of the over $35,000 Joseph was thought to have taken from his safety deposit box before his escape.

Transfer forms were signed and Louis Buono, Joseph's former friend and colleague, escorted him back to Pennsylvania with all the formality befitting a dangerous, captured convict. A crowd of 200 onlookers were at the penitentiary to see Joseph Bruno returned to prison. Joseph was led into the penitentiary as Cecilia and Antoinette looked on secretly from their Packard. Joe would be rendered the same procedure and quarantine as his family members had endured many months earlier. Once inside the regular prison, he was assigned the prison number D-2381.

During his internment, Joseph was assigned to Block 11 with the rest of his family and given no special privileges. However, he was occasionally able to conduct some operations with outside contacts. Antoinette continued to run the business except on a much smaller scale. She and Cecilia visited the penitentiary every two weeks for the remaining years Joseph was incarcerated.

Joseph, however, was keenly aware that while he was in prison his family had to continue to be protected. But the danger of such protection crumbling hovers close by unless all the details are carried out properly. Revenge may be a beautiful thing, but it had to be done well. Because, if detected, it was useless and messy.

The bakery where Antoinette and her father had met was to be the site of such an act. A huge establishment located on Washington near South Street in Philadelphia, it was there that pizza shells and many delicious Italian delights were made. The plan was for the explosion to be as neat as possible, not leave any evidence that would point to anyone remotely associated with Joseph Bruno.

Anthony was to drop the small package by the side of the flour sacks which would be piled on the loading dock at 4:45 am. It was important not to be late—once the sacks were left on the dock, the morning bakers would arrive within thirty minutes to haul them inside. If the bomb went off in ten minutes, as planned, no one would get hurt, except for Johnny who lived upstairs and was the target anyway. Johnny was always thought to have been the man who drove away in the yellow car after firing the first shots on that fateful night.

Everything went as planned. The timing was exact. The damage was excessive, however, and the bakery would never open again. The place was gutted by the time the fire department made it to the scene. There was no evidence, nothing left to sift through.

The only hitch was that Johnny was not dead. The bomb had been planted and everything went as planned except Johnny did not open the door to the dock as was his daily routine. He had

232 • Bruce Boyd

gone out the front door to check on his new car, and when the explosion took place Johnny was sheltered by the garage next door. He did, however, have severe injuries. He would never hear again from his left ear, and he would not be able to stand the lengths of time that were needed to run a bakery.

Other attempts at revenge or retribution were made over the years while Joseph was in jail. However, once all the newspapers and rumors stopped retelling the events, most people in the village and nearby towns began to forgive those involved. By the late 1940's, few people really remembered what had actually happened and what was rumor.

As the younger sons and nephews were released, some early on parole, life started to resume once again, but it would never get back to normal. Joseph's health continued to deteriorate as his Bright's Disease progressed. His attorneys tried unsuccessfully in 1946 to get him released on a pardon from the governor. It was not to be, not with the Democrats still holding all the power.

The years passed slowly and Joseph's influence in Pennsylvania weakened. He had few connections in politics and most of his businesses were long gone. Antoinette carried on with the few that were still active. The money was mostly gone, as well. The costly trials, escape, and attempts at pardons had all caused the dwindling of the financials of the once-wealthy family.

The sons, as a condition of their paroles, all had regular jobs, as well as some of the funds that Joseph had set aside for each one years earlier. Joseph's two daughters owned some land and, of course, they still had the house. Cecilia was kept away from the financial aspects of their lives so she never had to deal with that burden. Antoinette made sure that her mother was well taken care of and didn't want for anything, except her Joseph.

EPILOGUE

Following the Second World War, when the Republican Party took over once again, the state of Pennsylvania elected James Dorr as governor. One of his first acts on Christmas Eve, December 24th, 1947, was to issue a pardon for Joseph James Bruno and the members of his family who had spent time in prison. On January 17, 1948, Joseph finally went home to Kelayres.

By that time, Joseph was very ill, his health having failed. His advanced kidney disease had weakened him considerably. He had trouble standing for any length of time. But he never lost his fighting spirit or lowered his stature. When he walked out of the Eastern State Penitentiary as a free man after twelve years, he told the reporters waiting outside the gate that he was thinking of running for public office again, "if things worked out."

One day, sometime later, a man knocked on the door of the brick house on the corner. Some schoolboys were passing by. They watched and listened as the man, on his knees at the door, pleaded, "I must see Joseph Bruno! Please, let me see him!"

A woman answered softly, "No, I am sorry. It's impossible. He is very tired and is resting with his family."

"But I must! It's very important that he hears what I must say! Please!"

Joseph heard the man's piteous plea and came to the door, walking slowly, leaning on his cane. The man crawled on his knees to reach Joseph's outstretched hand. He looked old to the boys, still watching, fifty years or more, yet he could barely compose himself enough to speak.

Finally, the boys heard him say, "Mr. Bruno, I am so sorry. I did not mean to hurt you and your family. They told me I had to say what I said or my life would be worthless. I had no choice! Please, sir! You must forgive me! I must repay you somehow."

Joseph was silent for a moment, then said, "There is nothing that you must do. You did what you thought was right for you and your family at the time. Now you will have to live with that. I cannot forgive you or punish you. That is only up to the Lord." Joseph paused to catch his breath. Standing for that long and speaking that much was hard for him.

Then he continued, "Pray. Pray. That is all I can tell you— pray for your soul and perhaps the Lord will forgive you. I am but a mortal man, who has paid dearly for the sins of others. I am not well, I am not of this world for much longer. You do not have to fear me. Go to your family now. I am going back inside to mine."

The school boys walked on, amazed that the man, Mr. Bruno, still had so much power over the people in the village. Many more such people who had spoken falsely at the trials tried to seek forgiveness from the man that they had tried to ruin, from a family they had tried to bring down by smearing its name.

The lives of the Bruno family members changed completely. They became reclusive and quiet. Their day-to-day living became modest. Gradually people started to forget the bad times, or at least to let bygones be bygones. Some of the women of the town seemed to understand. Many people remained loyal, remembering what the family had done for them.

People brought them food, coal and some firewood, a little fruit, a basket of vegetables. All the damages to the house were eventually repaired.

Joseph lived his last few years quietly, never really regaining his strength, never again running for office. But he was not a broken man, only tired, and ill, and through it all he walked tall and proud, chest out, shoulders back, and he taught all his grandchildren to do the same.

Joseph James Bruno died at the big house on the corner of Centre and Fourth Streets in Kelayres, Pennsylvania, on July 7th, 1951. He was surrounded by his family, his children and his grandchildren.

Cecilia, Joseph's wife, that lovely young girl who had won his heart, whom he had married when they were both still but children, continued to live in the house he had built for her. She died there on February 17, 1959, with her daughters by her side. She left the house to both of them. Elveda lived in it with her husband Mickey until they died. Antoinette received some land on the mountainside of McAdoo Heights.

Antoinette returned to teaching and taught for many years. She found love again, and though the match may not have been a fairytale romance, she was happy and she loved her new husband Harold very much. Her grandchildren called him Grandpa. When Antoinette's two daughters grew up, they both married and moved to opposite ends of the country.

When the men were released from prison they were required to work at regular jobs and to have no contact with their former associates or former ways of earning money. Jimmy went to work at a clothing mill, where he met the woman who became his wife. They married and had a son they named James, continuing the tradition of his grandfather who had emigrated from Italy.

One evening when the family was sitting at dinner in the big brick house, a knock on the door was heard. A young man stood there, looking somewhat familiar.

"Is this where the Brunos live?" he asked.

"Yes," he was told, and asked why he wanted to know.

The young man said that his mother, who now lived in Colorado, had told him his father was Jimmy Bruno. Apparently, he was Jimmy's child by Carmine, his long-lost love. The family all agreed that he was the image of their Jimmy.

When Jimmy heard that his old love had borne his child, his anger returned, intensified, and he took his family and went to Baltimore, Maryland, where he spent the rest of his life, breaking completely with his father. He is the only Bruno not buried in the family plot in Kline Township.

Ernie finished his private school education and stayed home near his mother. With his part of Joseph's Bruno's estate, Ernie bought Jimmy's house and moved into it with his wife Mary. He also bought a tractor-trailer rig. Sadly, Ernie died at the age of 40 in an accident involving his truck and an automobile.

James Biaggio Bruno had dreamed a dream that grew, came true, but then died. The success he had fought so hard to attain, had worked so hard to earn, was destroyed one sad, dark night in Kelayres, Pennsylvania. James left his home in Italy, where life had been so difficult, and started a new life in America. He brought his family with him, held tightly to the tradition of family ties and carried all that was dear to him from the tiny town of Bucita in Italy to the little village of Kelayres in America.

Today, no one named Bruno lives in Kelayres. The descendants of James Biaggio Bruno are scattered across the country. The town that the Bruno brothers once claimed for themselves—built, owned and helped name, run by them and their sons and grandsons for many years—now shows barely a trace of their presence. Yet if one looks closely at the stonework over the main entrance of the old schoolhouse, one can still see beneath the newly carved "Kelayres School" the almost obliterated words "Bruno School"—a visual reminder of how the family's influence in the town of Kelayres also faded over the years.

As James Biaggio Bruno had said back in Italy,

"...this was his home, his family's home and it had been so for generations. Not just the home of his parents and brothers and sisters, but of his grandparents, his aunts and uncles, his cousins, great-uncles and great-aunts, second cousins, cousins by marriage— too many to name. They joked about being related to everyone in the village. And half of the next village. You always knew you could get help with your problems because the family was always there.

"But there was only so much the family could do when life was so hard, when everyone had to struggle for every little bit, every bite of food, every tool, every scrap of clothing.

Why? Why did it always have to be so hard?"

Sources

Books:
Bernard, Clyde. *Kelayres Massacre and History of Bruno Corruptible Political Reign.* **N.p., n.d.**
Hoover, Stephanie. *The Kelayres Massacre.* Charleston: The History Press, 2014.

Article:
Cerullo, John, Gennaro Deena. "The Kelayres Massacre," *Pennsylvania Magazine of History and Biography*, vol. 107, number 3, July 1, 1938. Print.

Newspapers:
Chicago Tribune

Hazelton Plain Speaker

New York Times

Philadelphia Inquirer

Pottsville Republican

Standard Sentinel (Hazelton, Pennsylvania)

Personal Letter:
Antoinette Bruno Billig

Nanny [Antoinette Bruno Billig] wrote this in response to an article in 1984 on the 50th anniversary of the Kelayres Massacre. Nanny gave this to me when she found out I was researching at the Hazelton Library. She said this was the truth of what happened that dreadful day, and she had saved it for just that reason—to right the wrongs that had been reported.

Bruce Boyd

After reading your flaunting article regarding the Kelayres regretful incident of 1934, let me give you my version of the occurrence. Believe me I was there! There isn't a shred of truth in your interpretation of the Event. Both parties Republicans and Democrats had a meeting—the Democrats were at a positive state of defeat! The Republican meeting adjourned and everyone left, all was well, we went to our homes, etc.!

The Democrats who were easily daunted by . . . lies, deception, intimidation, etc. were easily convinced because of their lack of the English language and education, which played an important persuasive factor, in their involvement. The elders who still live in Kelayres can verify any part of this statement, how the Democrats were all aroused over misinformation and the fear of losing the election. They were in a state of maniac confusion, started down the street yelling, screaming. As they neared the Bruno home they were an uncontrollable mob. They began to throw stones, coal, pot lids, wooden pieces, etc.! One man . . . yelled lets rusha [sic] the house. This was taking place on the front of the Bruno home, while on the side (4th Street) were some of the mob. One of them . . . who had a gun upraised and saw James Bruno a son of Joseph who lived next to his fathers' house exit from his home to attempt to enter his father's from the rear door. When James tried to enter a man . . . cried out, there goes a Bruno and fired a shot. James was not hit! Because of God's intervention! All was quiet in the Bruno home, the first shots were fired outside. Joseph Bruno was in his own home with his wife, children, and grand-children! Place yourself in these circumstances. How would you react?

Forgot to mention . . . across the street was shooting from his front porch with a shotgun. Then shots came from the Bruno home in response. Second floor bedroom windows were shattered by stones thrown by the mob. The first shots were fired outside the Bruno home! Many witnesses say that shots were fired across the mob from the corner opposite the Bruno home, perhaps hitting the crowd.

Joseph Bruno was an honorable man, he served the town faithfully as a school director for many years, a director of The First National Bank of McAdoo, as a County Detective. Why would a leader in his community, a respected individual, throw away his life and all his accomplishments?

As a School Director he helped many children who had no shoes to attend school. He took the children of . . . of Kelayres, to McAdoo, bought each one a pair of shoes in Frank Kline's store! (Just one example, there's a lot more). As a Director of The First National Bank of McAdoo he paid the mortgage on the . . . property of Kelayres, when the bank was going to foreclose! As a County Detective there are numerous persons I could mention whom he put on the County relief rolls so they had enough to eat. What kind of man is that? Had he concern for his fellow man? Why would he bring home a hunting license for men who could not afford to get one! He went on Saturday and Sunday to the local baseball field at the edge of town to watch local boys. We knew every player on the team by name. I could go on and on.

That night it was no parade, it was a mob!

Editor's note – Various names have been removed from this letter.

Bruno Family Tree

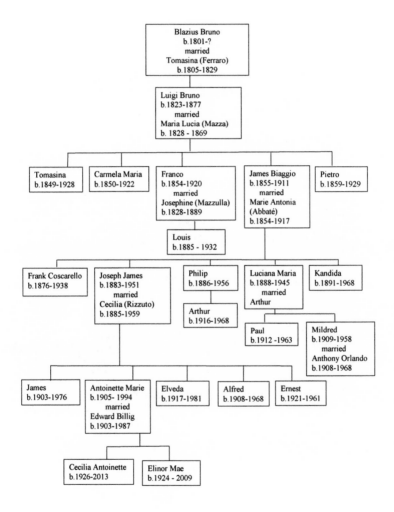

CPSIA information can be obtained
at www.ICGtesting.com
Printed in the USA
FFOW05n1843091116

9 781532 320200